# THE FOUR DAYS OF WATERLOO

LUC DE VOS

# THE FOUR DAYS OF WATERLOO

*The 15th, 16th, 17th and 18th June 1815*

**Photographic work :** Bernard Compagnion


The Dutch-language version of this work is published under the title *"Het einde van Napoleon, Waterloo 1815"*

Copyright Éditions Versant Sud
Place Verte 63/404
B-1348 Louvain-la-Neuve


D 2002/9445/4
ISBN 2-930358-03-3


Printed in Belgium

# ACKNOWLEDGEMENTS

We wish to thank Captain B. Janssens, Captain J.-M. Sterken-dries and Lieutenant W. Steurbaut for their assistance in the preparation of this work. We are also indebted to the Wellington Museum, the Musée de l'Armée and the Musée d'Armes de Liège for having kindly made their collections and prints available to us.

Juillet 2002
cadeau de Anouck Hermans.

# Foreword

No battlefield has been described as extensively as Waterloo. The French, the British, the Germans and the Dutch all have their own versions of what took place there. This is largely due to the paucity of accurate sources, to the different nationalities of the witnesses, and to linguistic divisions. The myth created around the battle is explicable in terms of the romanticism which followed the Napoleonic era. Well-known authors such as Victor Hugo, Stendahl, Erckmann-Chatrian and Byron describe the events that contributed to the creation of the many legends. On the French side, the most blatant departure from the truth consists in blaming the defeat on Grouchy's alleged treachery. Napoleon's memoires do not throw any light on the subject, and neither do the many controversies. The British present the battle as though they alone had gained the victory whereas, in fact, they had no hope of success without the Prussian intervention. Also, two thirds of Wellington's army consisted of Germans, Dutch and "Belgians". The Germans seem to say that only Blücher's loyalty made Wellington's victory possible, but the Prussians' doubts and hesitations about intervening are swept under the carpet. At the present time, French-speaking Belgians are leaning more and more towards the Napoleonic myth. They are overwhelmed by the cultural imperialism of Paris to such an extent that the late Henri Bernard, my eminent predecessor, was alone in adopting the British thesis. Certain hotheads would even like to do away with the Lion. A colleague went as far as to write in the *Dictionnaire d'Histoire de Belgique*, published under the direction of Hervé Hasquin, that "Belgians took part in the Battle of Waterloo, but mainly in the French army !" The Dutch and the Flemish seem to have little interest in the battle. The Belgian army has no tradition of the titanic struggle. In Dutch there are no publications worthy of the name that deal with the battle.

The number of Belgians who fought in the armies facing each other at Waterloo has never been reliably established. Various studies have been undertaken to solve this problem but, for one reason or another, they have always been very incomplete. Today, however, a figure can be put forward which must be close to reality. Of the 70,000 men present at Waterloo on the French side, it would seem that 1,350 "Belgians" (including many officers) participated in the battle. Research has also been undertaken into the allied units. In their case, the numbers suggested are more open to discussion than in the case of the French. André Bikar produces evidence to support his outright rejection of the claims made by Bas and t'Serclaes de Wommerson. In his view the *Zuid Nederlander* battalions that fought at Waterloo were not made up exclusively of "Belgians". The strength of the *Zuid Nederlander* units was 4,315 men. A study of all the documents available suggests 3,600 "Belgian" soldiers in the Allies' service to be nearest to the mark. But nothing is less certain !

International interest in the battlefield owes a lot to what was at stake. The result at Waterloo put an end to an era and removed the French from centre stage. Britain emerged as a leading power and the way was open for Prussia to play a major role in Germany and, indeed, in Continental Europe. The progress of liberalism was temporarily blocked, but the *ancien régime* was not restored. The Congress of Vienna, inaugurated shortly before the battle, was the first serious attempt at problem solving. Today, the 18th June 1815 is an important date in history as, indeed, is the 18th June 1940, when General Charles de Gaulle called upon his fellow-countrymen to continue the struggle.

The fact that the battlefield lies close to Brussels and arouses interest throughout the world encouraged us to undertake a study which takes account of the points of view of the countries directly engaged in the drama of Waterloo. We also attempt to set down our personal interpretation and appreciation. The fact that Napoleon's fate was sealed in Belgium is once more proof of the central role played by our country in the history of Western Europe.

*Brussels-Louvain, 18<sup>th</sup> June 1996*

# Methods of fighting in 1815

Napoleon envisaged two basic methods of engaging his troops in combat, namely manoeuvering along internal axes of movement, and cutting the enemy lines of communication. This is why it was vital to march separately but to fight together. When Napoleon used manoeuvering along internal axes against a numerically stronger enemy, this consisted of attacking his various numerically weaker opponents one by one. In this way he could always enjoy the local advantage of numbers. While their comrades were locked combat, weak French shadowing formations endeavoured to keep uncommitted enemy troops at bay by exploiting the terrain, and particularly its aquatic features.

*A British "India Pattern" infantry musket (Collection of the Musée d'Armes de la ville de Liège).*

The facts that Napoleon almost always had to fight against coalitions and that contemporary France was the most heavily populated country in Europe were of great significance in his manoeuvering along internal axes as, indeed, were the *levée en masse* and the conscription that he ordered.

Cutting lines of communication was a tactic frequently used by the French armies at the beginning of the Revolution, and particularly against numerically weaker foes. XVIII century armies were paralysed if their umbilical cords were cut, as it were. From the very beginning the French revolutionary armies lived off the land. The Prussians, the Austrians and the Dutch followed the French example. The British, however, continued to cling to their lines of communication which, in the majority of cases, extended back to at least one seaport. Napoleon very often cut his opponents' lines of communication to force them to fight in reverse order and on ground of his choice.

Marching in separate columns — mostly of army corps size — was an essential part of operations. The main line of advance was cleared and looting facilitated, yet the troops could be concentrated in plenty of time. An army corps had everything that it needed to operate independently and could involve itself in separate small engagements if the need arose. For Napoleon, marching, fighting and pursuit were all a matter of permanent movement.

Wellington was not a strategist in the real sense of the term, and his talent as a commander only showed itself at tactical level. He always endeavoured to fight on ground selected by himself, choosing defensive action behind a concentric fold in the ground.

To estimate the distances that had to be covered by the various bodies of troops of an army marching towards a battle, it is extremely important to know the minimum length of a battle itself. At the beginning of the XIX century a battle fought by an army of between 50,000 and 100,000 men lasted at least six hours.

Tactics always depend heavily upon the type of armament available and each arm — infantry, cavalry and artillery — has its own types of approach. We will therefore examine the armament and tactics employed by the different arms.

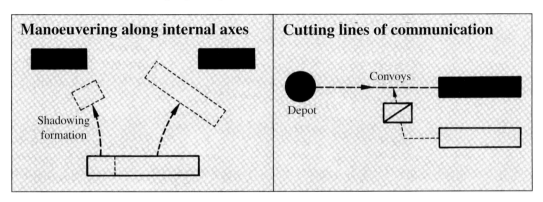

**Manoeuvering along internal axes**

Shadowing formation

**Cutting lines of communication**

Convoys

Depot

*The 1777 model*
*French infantry musket*
*(MRA collection).*

The infantry was equipped with a flintlock musket, a single-shot weapon requiring priming to fire [1]. These weapons fired spherical lead bullets and were smoothbore except for the far from common *Baker* rifle and Prussian *Buksen.* Loading was carried out as follows. The soldier extracted a cartridge from his cartridge pouch, tore off the end with his teeth and shook a little of the powder — about a gramme — into the pan adjacent to the touch-hole. He then closed the pan, poured the rest of the powder down the barrel, and inserted the ball and some of the cartridge paper as a wad. These were rammed home with the ramrod. To fire the soldier pulled back the cock holding the flint and opened the pan. He then pressed the trigger and the flint struck against the steel forming part of the pan-cover. This produced a shower of sparks that ignited the small quantity of powder in the pan. Passing through the touch-hole, the flame reached the 10 grammes or so of powder in the barrel. The resulting explosion despatched the ball along the bore.

The *1777 model* French musket in its Year IX and XIII [2] versions was in use in most of the Belgian units in the service of the Kingdom of the Netherlands. It weighed 4.375 kilos, had a

---

1. We recommend B. P. HUGHES' *"Firepower"* (London 1974) on the subject of the firearms of the age. There is a 1777 model musket in the Musée Royal de l'Armée in Brussels.
2. Year IX: from 23rd September 1800 to 22nd. September 1801. Year XIII: from 23rd September 1804 to 22nd September 1805.

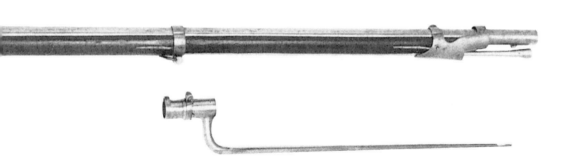

length of 1.515 metres, a calibre of 17.55 mm, and its ball weighed 21 grammes. This large calibre was particularly effective against horses. The recoil was powerful, however, and this did not help aiming. It was possible to fire about one shot a minute, but 20% were misfires. In heavy rain these weapons would not fire at all, and firing in high winds was ruled out because the powder was blown out of the pan. The flint in its lead mounting had to be changed every 30-50 shots.

The barrel rapidly fouled up and had to be cleaned out with the ramrod every 50 or 60 shots. The powder was threequarters saltpeter, an eighth of sulphur and an eighth of relatively coarse-grained charcoal with some 300-400 grains to a gramme. The maximum range of the French musket was 900 metres at an elevation of 45 degrees, but its effective range in combat was scarcely 40. Each infantryman carried 30-35 ball cartridges in his pouch.

British, Dutch and a certain number of German units were equipped with the *Longland India Pattern,* the so-called *Brown Bess,* which had a calibre of 19.3 mm (.75) and fired a 32 gramme (1 ounce) ball with a diameter of 18.03 mm. The stopping power of this weapon was much greater than that of its French counterpart. It was less accurate, however, and lacked both a front and a back sight because of its greater windage. This musket could thus be loaded more rapidly, at a rate of some 2 rounds a minute. Between 1793 and 1815 three million were mass-produced, a number which greatly exceeding the figure for the French weapon. Some authors claim that the British musket had fewer misfires, some 5 % only. Each soldier carried 50 ball cartridges in his pouch.

The Prussian musket, which was manufactured at the Potsdam-Spandau and the Neisse-Malapane arms factories, was a virtual copy of the 1803 version of the French 1777 model. It had a calibre of 18.57 mm and a breech end fitted with a blade. This made it possible to cut off the cartridge ends and so to avoid the tiresome process of tearing them off with the teeth. The Prussians could therefore load more rapidly and fire three shots a minute. This gadget also counterbalanced a relatively simple piece of self-mutilation consisting of damaging the front teeth to avoid military service. Certain units from Hanover, Brunswick and Nassau were equipped with a *Jãger* type of hunting rifle. All these weapons had to be cleaned out regularly with the ramrod.

Almost all the muskets were equipped with a long 40-cm bayonet with a triangular cross-section.

Skirmishers, who deployed in front of the main body of troops, fired individually. Their tactic, known as "Indian fighting", consisted of making maximum use of the terrain. Its inspiration came from the American revolutionaries, who had learnt it from the native population. A certain number of skirmishers had rifled weapons. These were more accurate, but loading was hard labour.

Line infantry was intended for shock action and fired in volleys at a range of some 40 metres, initially by battalion and later by company. This led to the battlefield being swathed in smoke. There then followed a brief and savage assault with the bayonet.

Despite the underlying order of things the British, with their small professional army, swore by lighter formations — a factor which did not prevent their being well structured in depth. They thus deployed their infantry in two ranks so as to be able to maintain maximum firepower. They had the habit of waiting for the attacking infantry to approach before firing at short range. A short and powerful counter-attack, punctuated by three "hurrahs", drove the attackers back. The attack brought up short after a few hundred metres, however. Against cavalry the best form of defence was to form squares, mostly of battalion size. The men were arrayed three or four ranks deep, with the gunners seeking shelter in the centre. Cannon might be posted at the four corners. The different squares (carrés, Karrees) were arranged diagonally or in checkerboard fashion so that they could provide covering fire for each other. The infantry fired at the horses.

There were two classes of cavalry. The light cavalry were hussars, *chasseurs à cheval*, and lancers (in the case of the

*The Quatre-Bras crossroads, the key to the Brussels and Namur roads, belatedly taken by the French on the 17th June (Lithograph by Jobard after Madou. MRA collection).*

17

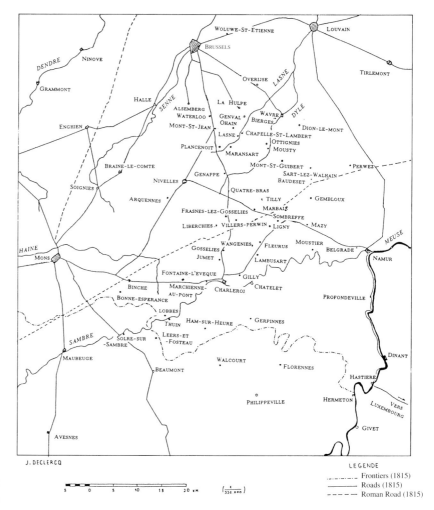

The map labels (as visible):

WOLUWE-ST-ÉTIENNE · LOUVAIN · BRUSSELS · NINOVE · DENDRE · OVERIJSE · LASNE · TIRLEMONT · GRAMMONT · HALLE · SENNE · LA HULPE · ALSEMBERG · WATERLOO · GENVAL · WAVRE · BIERGES · DYLE · OHAIN · MONT-ST-JEAN · DION-LE-DONT · ENGHIEN · LASNE · CHAPELLE-ST-LAMBERT · PLANCENOIT · OTTIGNIES · MOUSTY · MARANSART · BRAINE-LE-COMTE · MONT-ST-GUIBERT · PERWEZ · GENAPPE · SART-LEZ-WALHAIN · SOIGNIES · NIVELLES · BAUDESET · QUATRE-BRAS · ARQUENNES · TILLY · GEMBLOUX · MARBAIS · FRASNES-LEZ-GOSSELIES · SOMBREFFE · LIBERCHIES · VILLERS-PERWIN · LIGNY · MAZY · WANGENIES · FLEURUS · MOUSTIER · MEUSE · HAINE · GOSSELIES · BELGRADE · MONS · JUMET · LAMBUSART · NAMUR · FONTAINE-L'EVEQUE · GILLY · BINCHE · MARCHIENNE-AU-PONT · CHARLEROI · CHATELET · BONNE-ESPERANCE · PROFONDEVILLE · LOBBES · THUIN · HAM-SUR-HEURE · GERPINNES · LEERS-ET-FOSTEAU · SAMBRE · SOLRE-SUR-SAMBRE · DINANT · MAUBEUGE · WALCOURT · BEAUMONT · FLORENNES · HASTIERE · PHILIPPEVILLE · HERMETON · VERS LUXEMBOURG · GIVET · AVESNES

J. DECLERCQ

*The road network
in 1815.*

5  0  5  10  15  20 KM   ($\frac{1}{330\,000}$)

LEGENDE
.._.._.._ Frontiers (1815)
_____ Roads (1815)
- - - - - Roman Road (1815)

Prussians, Ulhans). As a rule the light cavalry was used for reconnaissance, the interception or escort of despatches, cutting lines of communication, providing close cover — particularly of the flanks — pursuit and foraging. The heavy cavalry consisted of dragoons, carabiniers with their metal breasplates, cuirassiers and gendarmes, and was deployed as shock troops or for possible breakthroughs. Charges against infantry took place in columns, and against cavalry in dispersed order.

18

The gallop started between 70 and 100 metres from the enemy. The riders crouched down over the sides of their horses, whose bodies protected them. In the light cavalry the principal weapon was the short sabre, and in the heavy cavalry the sword. Everybody had a firearm — in most cases a carbine, but a pistol in some, particularly the cuirassiers. The carbine was generally fitted with a bayonet. Some formations, including the Ulhans, were armed with lances.

On the battlefield there was an advanced level of cooperation between the cavalry and the infantry. When the heavy cavalry was attacking, the infantry followed a short distance behind. They made use of the cover and could step in if the charge failed. When the infantrywas attacking, the light cavalry protected the flanks against enfilading fire. If the infantry fell back, the cavalry charged in to assist them.

The artillery was equipped with bronze smooth-bore muzzle-loading cannon between 1.6 and 2.3 metres in length, and morters measuring at most 0.70 m. Their weights ranged from 200 kilos to a ton. The shot was of solid metal and varied between four and twelve pounds, and calibres were in function of the weight of the shot. The rate of fire could not exceed two shots a minute so as to prevent the premature and uncontrolled explosion of the charge caused by the heating of the barrel. After each shot the elevation had to be reset and the cannon returned to the firing position after recoiling between one and two metres.

There was a risk of the barrel exploding after some 500 shots. The British army allowed 180 rounds per cannon, and the French between 168 and 203. Firing was by line of sight, and this is why the cannon were place forward of the troops. During approach marches they fired in the spaces between the units on their side. Firing ceased just before the troops deployed to attack. The horse artillery provided support from the flanks, and only mortars were used to fire over the heads of friendly troops. As in the case of the cavalry, Napoleon concentrated a

*Uniforms from left to right : A Chasseur à Cheval of the Guard and a French infantry colonel ; a British grenadier of the 92nd Foot (Gordon Highlanders).*

considerable portion of his artillery. It was his *ultima ratio*. As for Blücher, he spread his artillery over his whole line. Artillery was employed mainly against infantry, and rarely against enemy artillery. Different calibres were used, with the heaviest guns having a range of 1,800 metres and an effective range of no more than 800.

Four fifths of the projectiles employed were solid cast-iron balls that could be reused or fired from larger-bore cannon if the need arose. When the weather was dry and the terrain flat, a ball fired straight and level or at a slight elevation hit the ground and bounced once or twice, cutting down every living thing in its path. These balls were used at ranges of between 300 and 500 metres and were very effective against infantry moving in close order since they generally killed between three and six men and wounded four or five. Between two and nine balls linked by a chain could be loaded into a small-bore cannon. This made for more reliable shooting but cut out the ricochets.

Canister was used at short ranges not exceeding 300 metres. The canisters were made of thin metal and contained a large number of small balls which fanned out as they left the

gun. Canister was very effective at short range against men and horses. The British six-pounder cannon fired 85 42-gramme or 41 88-gramme balls.

Mortars fired shells. These were spherical metal projectiles that exploded on impact, with the splinters producing the desired effect. Mortars enabled firing to take place over the heads of friendly troops.

*An officer of the 2nd Light Dragoons of the King's German Legion ; an NCO of the Dutch Horse Artillery ; a sergeant of a flank company of the Southern Dutch infantry in 1815 (MRA collection).*

Shrapnel and rockets were two typically British weapons. Britain was, after all, the home of the industrial revolution. Hadn't she also found inspiration in her colonies ? Shrapnel was the invention of Henry Shrapnel (1784) a British colonel. It came in the form of a shell containing between 27 and 85 metal balls, and the art lay in setting the explosive charge to go off in the air so that the balls were projected outwards and onwards. This weapon was used at long ranges of between 600 and 1,300 metres. At 900 metres the shrapnel covered an area 135 metres. As for *Congreve's rockets*, these were manufactured on a very limited scale. They had a range of over 2 kms, but their inaccuracy was proverbial. At Waterloo the British set up a battery of this type under Edward Whyniates.

Due to the coloured uniforms a battle could be followed from a distance with a telescope, but the amount of artillery smoke spoilt the view. Orders, either written or verbal, were carried by staff officers. In Napoleon's case these officers were often generals, whose rank gave them the necessary authority. Several riders were despatched simultaneously over long distances to ensure that a message arrived. Claude Chappe's optical telegraph was also used to transmit information. At the height of a battle orders were identifiable by the sound of flutes or trumpets. Commanding officers were accompanied by trumpeters, recognisable by their special uniforms. Series of pre-arranged calls gave the signal to attack, to retreat or to regroup. Apart from the trumpets, fifes and drums were the most widespread musical instruments.

A medical service barely existed. Stomach wounds were the most feared. The idealogical wars at the end of the century were considerably more brutal than the XVIII century's limited dynastic conflicts.

Only the British had a commissariat worthy of the name. They paid for the food supplies that they obtained, and were the only ones to find what they needed. As for the French, the Prussians and the troops of the Kingdom of the Netherlands, when they marched in the population fled with all their possessions, and anything that was left was looted. It was principally the supply of water that caused insurmountable problems since dirty surface water caused numerous diseases. Because of the lack of oats the horses were put out to graze, but too much grass did not seem to suit them. Apart from ox-carts, the commissariat also used boats on the many waterways.

*Chanlaire and Capitaine's map used by Napoleon.*

Soldiers set off to war laden like mules, with each man carrying some 30 kilos. The uniform with its high collar was anything but practical. The rain ran off the shako and down the back of the neck. The leather footwear, identical for either foot, hardly lasted for for 200 kms.

Maps were rare and expensive, and few officers could read them. For our provinces there was the 1796 map by Chanlaire and Capitaine — a slightly modified version of the Austrian map by Ferraris. Armies moved very slowly, with the infantry

*The Eagle lands ;*
*Napoleon arrives at the*
*Tuileries on the*
*20th March 1815.*

progressing cross-country and mostly no faster than 2.5 kilometres an hour. The artillery had to use the waterways and the few paved roads dating back to the time of Maria-Theresa and Joseph II. The cavalry and supply train usually followed these same roads. Bridges were generally narrow. They were frequently made of wood and could be burnt, but the stone ones were difficult to destroy and had to be dismantled. A bridge was often the prize in a hard-fought battle. Because of the lack of viable roads and the need to avoid interminably long columns, divisions very often marched cross-country side by side. Even so, a 6,000 man division formed a column 5 kms long.

All armies had spies, whose task it was to describe the morale of the enemy, both military and civil, to seek out information on his weaponry and to determine his strength, etc. Detailed studies were also made of the terrain over which operations would take place. Apart from the cryptographic department Napoleon's intelligence services generally worked well, and it was these services that had been behind France's most magnificent victories pre-1814. One of the best-known French spies was Charles-Louis Schulmeister, an Alsatian smuggler and businessman who did sterling work in his new post under General Anne (Jean Marie René) Savary, the Director of the Gendarmerie and Minister of Police (1810-14). This valuable spy was not at Waterloo. It is almost certain that at that time Schulmeister was Napoleon's secret emissary to Marie-Louise. Since an attempt to kidnap the Aiglon had been attributed to him — perhaps wrongly — Schulmeister was sought throughout the whole of Austria.

CHAPTER II

# Napoleon returns

Although abdicating under the terms of the agreement signed at Fontainebleau on the 9<sup>th</sup> April 1814, Napoleon was able to retain his title of emperor. He was also granted sovereignity over the small island of Elba (223.5 sq. kms.) some ten kilometres off the coast of Italy, of which it now forms part. He also received an annual pension of two million francs and had a personal guard of a thousand men. As for Marie-Louise, she received the duchies of Parma, Piacenza and Guastalla.

Due to his political blunders Louis XVIII had caused widespread dissatisfaction in France. The property of the Church and the aristocracy had been confiscated after the revolution and sold off cheaply. The farming community had profited greatly from these sales and now feared that the property would be returned to the Church and the nobles. The bourgeoisie were not satisfied with either the economic situation or the fact that they remained politically impotent. The imperial nobility took a dim view of the émigrés replacing them, and the large number of officers who had been sent home on half-pay dreamt nostalgically of the past. In Britain, the

27

liberal Whigs were not at all taken by Louis XVIII, whom they viewed as a reactionary. When he learnt that negotiations in Vienna were experiencing considerable difficulty and that agreement remained elusive, Napoleon decided to return to France. He left Porto Ferrajo on the 26th February 1815 on the brig *L'Inconstant* and, on the 1st. March, landed at Golfe-Juan, between Cannes and Antibes. The choice of this particular spot is significant. The Rhône valley was doubtlessly more convenient for a march to the north, but Napoleon feared the known royalism of the people living along it. He therefore chose the difficult route across the Alps to regain Paris. France hesitated. The 5th Regiment of Infantry was sent against him but could not resist his charisma and, on the 7th March, it changed sides just outside Grenoble. The following day Colonel Charles Huchet, Comte de la Bédoyère, came over at Vizille at the head of his regiment. He was the first senior officer to come out in favour of Napoleon. On the 9th March the garrison of Lyons raised the tricolour in the presence of the Comte d'Artois, the

*The main street of Waterloo. Wellington set up his headquarters opposite the church, in the inn owned by the widow Bodenghien. (Lithograph by Jobard after Madou, MRA collection).*

King's brother. Auxerre saw the 14th Regiment of Infantry switch to the Emperor on the 17th March, and on the 18th Marshal Michel Ney, the commander in chief of the royal army, rejoined his old commander at the head of 6,000 men. In Paris, people were becoming alarmed. Revolutionary slogans and songs were heard again. On the 19th, taking advantage of a dark night, Louis XVIII fled from Paris to Ghent. Twenty-one hours later Napoleon entered the Tuileries in the midst of an enthusiastic crowd on what was his son's birthday.

On the 7th March Vienna learnt of Napoleon's return to France. Shortly afterwards the news reached London and share values began to plummet on the Stock Exchange. The discord reigning between the powers rapidly evaporated in face of the resurgence of the common danger. Napoleon was outlawed by the eight powers — Austria, Britain, Portugal, Spain, Russia, Prussia, Sweden and France — in their declaration of the 13th March 1815. He was placed beyond the pale of civil and social relations and delivered to the vindication of public morality as an enemy and a disturber of universal peace and tranquility. With the exception of Sweden and Portugal, all the countries present at Vienna signed an offensive and defensive pact on the 25th March. On the 27th Tallyrand signed for France. Whatever happened, nobody was permitted to enter into a separate agreement with Napoleon. Starting on the 1st July, allied troops were to converge on Paris. Some 700,000 men from Austria, Prussia and Russia would be placed under the command of the Prince of Schwarzenberg. In the meanwhile the British and Prussians were to cover the Netherlands and the deployment of troops. On the 7th April Wellington was placed in command of the Anglo-Dutch forces. On the 3rd May Wellington and Blücher met at Tirlemont and decided to support each other in a possible defensive battle to the south or west of Brussels. At the insistance of the Prussians Wellington promised to launch an offensive in the direction of Mauberge on the 2nd July.

During this time Napoleon was taking the initiative. He announced to the Russians that they were the object of an agreement between the British, the Austrians and Louis XVIII. These three western powers feared the Russians' appetite (in relation to Poland). He sought his father-in-law's support. He hoped that the liberals would return to power in Britain. Had not Wellington's own brother come out against a war to impose a sovereign on a nation? He also announced that he would respect the Treaties of Paris of the 30th May 1814 and, consequently, the frontiers of the 1st November 1792 that they laid down. And in addition to everything else, he insisted on his peaceful intentions towards other countries and *vis-à-vis* his own public opinion.

In France, Napoleon was obliged to make some concessions. He abolished the censorship. In the *Acte Additionnel aux Constitutions de l'Empire* (22nd April) Benjamin Constant established the foundations of a liberal empire in which the bourgeoisie was allocated an important political role. From now on ministers would be responsible to parliament, whose debates would be public; a jury would deal with violations of the press laws, and religious worship would be free, etc. The low turnout of the qualified electorate (1.5 million out of 8) for the referendum on the *Acte Additionnel* showed Bonaparte how limited his room to manoeuvre was. This was even more evident with the make-up of the Lower Chamber and its two estates. Hard-core Bonapartists held barely a hundred seats. Most of the 629 deputies were liberals, who kept a watchful eye on the Emperor's doings. Napoleon tried to increase the number of his supporters by pardoning all those who had disowned him in 1814. He also wanted to attract the favour of the old aristocracy by reserving certain posts for them. The shakey bases of the Emperor's power would play a considerable part in the forthcoming campaign.

Napoleon's diplomatic position was made even more difficult by the inconsiderate attitude of Joachim Murat, his brother-in-law and King of Naples. As early as 1813 Murat had disowned Napoleon in the hope of saving his throne. He nevertheless took part in the German campaign at the

Emperor's side. But shortly afterwards — in January 1814 — he signed a treaty with Britain and Austria in which he declared that he had changed sides and promised to mobilise 30,000 men against his brother-in law. In the meanwhile he realised that the Bourbons were intending to take back the throne of Naples, and so began to talk of the liberation of Italy. On the 15th March he declared war on Austria, and marched on Rome at the head of 40,000 men ! The Pope fled and Bologna and Florence soon fell into Murat's hands. However, on the 2nd May he was beaten by the Austrians at Tolentinio. He fled to France, but Napoleon refused to accept him into his service. After the defeat at Waterloo Murat reached Corsica, from whence he embarked with a faithful few to attempt a landing in Calabria, in the south

*The Naveau mill at Fleurus, which served as Napoleon's observation post during the battle of Ligny (Lithograph by Williaume after Lignian (MRA collection).*

of Italy. He could not raise the population as he had hoped and soon fell into the hands of his enemies, who executed him on the 13th October.

From April 1815 it became clear to Napoleon that he would not be able to avoid a confrontation. Louis XVIII had abolished the unpopular conscription, known as the Law of Blood. Napoleon hesitated over reintroducing this law. On the 9th April he called for volunteers to rejoin the army. The interest on government loans suddenly dropped by eight points. The navy was converted into infantry and artillery and the National Guard was mobilised. On the 1st June an appeal was made to the 1815 levy, and Lazare Carnot once again tried to set up an army. At this juncture there were rumbles of revolt in a large part of France, a rising in the Vendée and civil war in the Midi, Bordeaux, Marseilles, Nîmes and Toulouse. Most of the clergy supported the Bourbons.

While Napoleon was endeavouring the rebuild an army, the powers were assembling their troops. The Emperor found himself on the horns of a dilemma. Should he wait for the enemy, recruit an army from the very large French population — 25 million at the time — and, by manoeuvering along internal axes, slow their advance ? Or should be defeat the allied forces of Britain, the Netherlands and Prussia by a lightening campaign in Belgium ? He considered that the former solution was difficult from a political point of view. The most patriotic provinces of Alsace, Lorraine and Champagne would be lost almost immediately. How would the liberals and the royalists react ? He remembered only too well how his own marshals had turned their backs on him in 1814 despite a whole series of victories. His Minister of War, Marshal Louis Davout, Prince of Eckmühl, was unreservedly in favour of the former solution. He thought that the general war-weariness and France's increasing military strength would cause the coalition to fall apart. Napoleon, however, believed that a rapid victory over Wellington and a large Prussian force would strengthen his hold on France and encourage the Austrians and Russians to negotiate. Furthermore, he hoped that the fall of Castlereagh's conservative government would follow. The fact that on the 25$^{th}$ May the House of Commons had approved the credits for the new campaign did not distract him from this conviction. A few days later he decided to attack the Netherlands.

In the meanwhile the shadowing forces had to be assembled which would keep the concentrically advancing enemy at bay. To the west of the Moselle and to the north of Luxembourg there were some 20,000 Prussians under the command of F. Kleist von Nellendorf, and there would soon be 124,000. Some 140,000 Russians under Mikhail Barcley de Tolly and Ferdinand Witzingerode were in the region of Heidelberg, on the Rhine. An Austro-German army of 210,000 men under K. von Schwarzenberg was occupying the region to the east of Bâle. With only 23,000 men at his disposal General Jean Rapp had to prevent them from reaching Nancy. The Jura corps, consisting of 8,400 men under Claude Lecourbe, was tasked with intercepting any attack by 37,000 Swiss under Bachmann. From Lyons, Marshal Louis Suchet's 23,000 strong Alpine corps was observing the Austro-Piedmontese army under J. von Frémont and Bianchi (50,000 men) deployed in Northern Italy. In the Var, Marshal Guillaume Brune was waiting with 5,500 men for the Napolitain army of 23,000 men under Onasco. Napoleon had placed two corps facing the 80,000 men of the Hispano-Portuguese army, one in the east (Toulouse) under C. Decaen with 7,000 men, and the other in the west (Bordeaux), with 6,800 men under B. Clausel. Jean-Maximilien Lamarque was to hold the Vendée with 10,000 men, and there were some 50,000 others spread throughout the rest of the country not counting the 20,000 in Paris under Davout.

As for the decisive campaign, this would be fought by the 121,000 men of the Northern Army who would meet the 106,000 British, Germans and Dutch under Wellington, who controlled the Scheldt, and the 117,000 Prussians under Blücher, who controlled the Meuse. The Prussian contribution was remarkable in view of the fact that the country had scarcely six million inhabitants, or about as many as the Kingdom of the Netherlands. Great Britain and Ireland, which had formed the United Kingdom since 1810, had some 15 million.

Most of the veterans who had fought with Wellington in the Iberian Peninsula were in Canada and part of the United States after taking part in the war between Britain and the United States which had ended in December 1814.

# CHAPTER III

# The opposing forces

## The Anglo-Dutch Army

Napoleon had no great opinion of Wellington. The defeats suffered by his lieutenants at the hands of the so-called "Sepoy General" made no real impression on him. Apart from age — 46 — and some dictatorial traits, the two men had little in common. In 1769 Arthur was born in Dublin into an Anglo-Irish family as the third son of Garret Wesley, the first Earl of Mornington. In 1798 the family changed its name to Wellesley. The future duke went to Eton, and also studied in Belgium and at the École Française d'Équitation in Angers. This enabled him to profit from the excellent military education founded by Louis XV. In 1787 he became an officer cadet, and thanks to money and patronage he was promoted lieutenant colonel in the 33rd Foot at the age of 25.

In this same year — 1794 — he was at the head a brigade that failed in an attempt to land in Zeeland. He then served in India from 1797 to 1805, and it was in India that he was promoted major general in 1802. During this time he was engaged in an unbroken series of minor wars and alliances, so acquiring the knowledge and experience that would stand him in good stead later on. Arthur Wellesley would become a

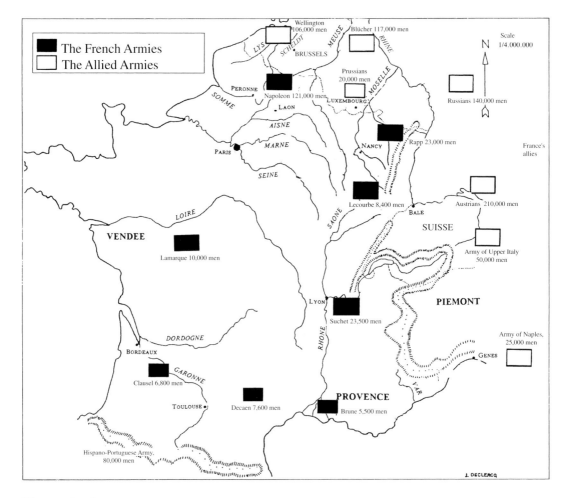

*The opposing forces.*

commander with a rational turn of mind and an aristocratic air who knew how to be tough, and who linked military competence with political acumen. Despite a certain pride he was liked by his men because he knew how to obtain victories and to take good care of the substance of his army, mainly recruited from the dregs of society.

After another voyage, during which he called in at St. Helena, we find him in the winter of 1805-06 commanding a brigade at the mouth of the Elbe. In 1806 he became a Member of Parliament and married. He then exercised some minor commands before being appointed Secretary of State for Ireland in a Tory cabinet. He opposed Catholic power but nevertheless agreed to pay the clergy in the hope of obtaining their loyalty to the state.

He was promoted lieutenant general in 1808, and shortly afterwards he was sent to Portugal at the head of an expeditionary force. An ally of Britain since the XIV century, Portugal persisted in refusing to cooperate in the continental blockade. Napoleon therefore decided on a punitive expedition that Britain would endeavour to counter. Faced with the extent of the French resources the British commander in chief came to an agreement with the French army, and a disappointed Wellington returned to London. In April 1809 he was back at the head of a new army. With the cooperation of the Portuguese, the remainder of the Spanish army and numbers of insurgents he succeeded on several occasions in beating separate French generals, and particularly André Masséna and Nicolas Soult. Now graced with the title of Duke of Wellington, he continued the struggle in the Peninsula beyond 1809. When Napoleon withdrew a large number of troops in 1812 for his attack on Russia, Wellington launched an unremitting offensive which, in 1814, would bring him to the gates of Toulouse. There he defeated Soult on the 10th April in the last battle of the war against France. In the meanwhile 1813 saw him promoted field marshal. The following year he became a member of the House of Lords and received a shower of titles. He was subsequently appointed Ambassador to Paris and the British representative at the Congress of Vienna.

During the Peninsula campaign Wellington more or less perfected his tactics such as taking up position behind a rise in the ground, the deployment of a screen of skirmishers making skilful use of the terrain, and the judicious positioning of his artillery, etc. He knew how to make maximum use of the firearms of the period and ordered volleys to be fired at short range only. Exploiting firmness and phlegm — two major traits of the British character — he drew up his troops in two lines whereas the enemy advanced in columns. He usually launched a brief counter-attack after ordering a murderous volley.

Wellington's many victories brought him unequalled popularity at a moment in history when France dominated Europe. And so he found himself in command of the army that was to clash with the Grand Master Napoleon for the first and, indeed, for the last time.

A certain time was required to set up the quadrilingual Anglo-Dutch army. The staff was limited in size and, in Wellington's view, its staff-work was not beyond reproach - before the battle at least. Prince William of Orange had been with Wellington for a certain time in Spain but, placed at the head of the 1st Corps at the age of 22, he could hardly be described as a great commander. However, he could always rely on the support of a brilliant chief of staff in the person of Baron Jean Victor de Constant-Rebeque, an ex-officer of Louis XVI's Swiss Guard. The commander of the 2nd Corps was the first-rate Lord Rowland Hill, who had received his baptism of fire at the siege of Toulon. The command of the cavalry was entrusted to Lord Arthur Paget, Earl of Uxbridge. The least that could be said was that this appointment lacked tact since Lord Uxbridge had absconded with Wellington's sister-in-law ! Certain of the divisional commanders were capable, and particularly Thomas Picton of the 5th division. Count Karl von Alten was the most experienced of the Hanoverians. Duke Frederick William commanded the troops from Brunswick. He had lost everything because of Napoleon — his father, his brother, his wife and his duchy. A certain number of the generals, including the Dutch David Chassé and the Belgian Jean de Collaert and Jean-Baptiste van Merlen, had earned their spurs in the French army.

The Anglo-Dutch army was approximately a third British, a third German with the King's German Legion and contingents from Hanover, Brunswick and Nassau, and a third from the new Kingdom of the Netherlands [3].

---

3. D. CHANDLER, *Waterloo. The hundred days*, London, 1980, p. 63.

|  | Infantry | Cavalry | Artillery | (guns) | Total |
|---|---|---|---|---|---|
| British Troops | 23,543 | 5,913 | 5,030 | (102) | 34,486 |
| King's German Legion | 3,301 | 2,560 | 526 | (18) | 6,387 |
| Hano-verians | 22,788 | 1,682 | 465 | (12) | 24,935 |
| Bruns-wickers | 5,376 | 922 | 510 | (16) | 6,808 |
| Nassau | 2,880 | — | — | — | 2,880 |
| Dutch and Belgians | 24,174 | 3,405 | 1,635 | (56) | 29,214 |
| Engineers Supply and staff officers (British) | – | – | 1,240 | (12) | 1,240 |
| Totals | 82,062 | 14,482 | 9,406 | (216) | 105,950 |

The British infantry and artillery were first-class The men were recruited from the urban proletariat. Significant material advantages and a taste for adventure attracted recruits. There was an attractive premium upon joining, pay above the wage of an unskillked labourer, and stable employment for 20 years. The heavy cavalry with its huge horses was one of the most magnificent in Europe. On the other hand, the light cavalry was not adequately trained for its duties — the collection of intelligence, the interception of despatches, and the

*Following pages : The commanders in chief were not afraid of exposing themselves in the front line. Wellington at Quatre-Bras (MRA collection).*

exploitation of the situation. The men adored Wellington, their commander in chief. Referring to his aquiline nose they called him *Old Hookey* or *Noosey*[4].

The King's German Legion was made up of men bought by Britain from German princes at a rate of £11 a man. It was a crack corps trained along British lines and under officers from both Britain and Germany.

The French-hating young troops from Brunswick in their black uniforms covered with insignia (including a death's head) had a terrifying appearance. The units from Orange-Nassau under the command of Prince Bernard of Saxe-Weimar were excellent.

On the other hand, the loyalty of a number of Dutch, Nassau and, particularly, Belgian units aroused a certain amount of doubt. Hadn't they served in the French army ? Half of the Dutch infantry, which was recruited on a regional basis, had never smelled the smell of powder.

The British artillery had 6- and 9-pounder cannon and 5.5-inch mortars. Some German units were equipped with French 4-6- 8- and 12-pounders and 6.5-inch mortars. The Dutch and the Belgians had French 6-pounders. The French pound corresponded to 1.1 British pounds, so that French 8-pounder was the same as a British 9-pounder.

Only the British had a commissariat worthy of the name. As for the medical service, it was virtually non-existent on the Anglo-Dutch side.

---

4. Probably an old spelling for Old Hooky and Nosey.

# The Prussian Army

The 72-year old Gebhard Leberecht Blücher von Wahlstatt was commander of the Prussian army west of the Rhine. He was a practical soldier, dynamic and extremely brave, and also a charismatic commander whose men treated him to such names as *Alter Vorwärts* (Old Man Forwards) and *Papa Blücher.*

Blücher was born in 1742 in Mecklenburg and started his career at the age of 14 in a Swedish cavalry regiment. After being captured by the Prussians he changed sides and became one of Frederick II the Great's officers. But his fits of anger, his gambling, women and drink led to his undoing, and he left the army in 1772.

After Frederick the Great's death he rejoined the Prussian army with the rank of major. As the result of his courage at Kaiserslautern he was promoted major general in 1794. He fought against the French unremittingly. His courage and tenacity led to his promotion to lieutenant general in 1806. After the defeats of Jena and Auerstedt on the 14th October he was leading the rearguard of the Prussian Guard when he fell into the hands of the French. A few days later he was exchanged for Marshal Claude Perrin, otherwise known as Victor, the future governor of Prussia. When Prussia was reduced to the status of a French satellite Napoleon made sure that Blücher was dismissed.

In 1813, after Prussia had thrown off the French yoke, Blücher became commander in chief in Silesia and so took part in the battles of Lützen and Bautzen, which heralded the French retreat from Silesia. In October 1813 he fought at Leipzig. During the French campaign he held Napoleon in check at Laon. His hatred of Napoleon was well known and, in 1815, he again took up arms.

In 1814 Britain honoured him, and it was from that moment that his warm feeling for the country dated. He was aware of his shortcomings. When in that year he was made an honorary doctor by Oxford University he promptly observed that von Gneisenau was at least worthy of the title of pharmacist since they complemented each other !

Count August Neithardt von Gneisenau was born in 1760 into an old Austrian family. He first of all served in Britain and America before joining the Prussian service in 1786. In 1807 he distinguished himself at the defence of Kolberg. He was dismissed the service in 1809 at Napoleon's insistence because of his association with Karl von Stein and Gerhard von Scharnhorst and his sympathy for the League of Virtue (*Tugendbund*). Having become a diplomat he spent time in Britain, but this only went to strengthen his youthful aversion for the country. Because of his haughty and obstinate manner this idealist and "gentleman" lost among the great reformers was not exactly appreciated by the mediocre King Frederick William III.

In 1813 Gneisenau became Blücher's chief of staff in Silesia. He occupied the same post during the French campaign in 1814, and again in 1815. He was the real strategist in the Prussian army, surrounding himself with a staff of intellectuals.

*A bronze French 6-pounder cannon manufactured at Douaire and captured at Waterloo. On loan to the Wellington Museum from the Royal Armouries, London.*

Together with Scharnhorst, Herman Boyen and Karl von Clausewitz he contributed to the forming of the new Prussian army.

A considerable part of the Prussian infantry was made up of elements of the *Landwehr*, or the territorial defence. This was an idea of G. von Scharnhorst (1755-1813), who wanted to "arm the people". He introduced short and generalised military service as a sort of exchange for freeing the peasantry from the feudal system. It was in this way that the *Landwehr* came into being. The bourgeoisie served in *Jäger* units. The army thus formed part of the nation and its bad reputation was mitigated. Patriotism was very fervent, and the Iron Cross was the decoration which appeared most frequently on the sober uniforms of the Prussian officers. The cavalry and artillery were not particularly large and were distributed over the brigades. Units from Westphalia and Saxony accepted Prussian authority only reluctantly.

The tactical units were the brigades, consisting of infantry, cavalry and artillery. Four brigades formed a corps. The Prussian army on the Lower Rhine was made up of four corps. Of these, the 1st was commanded by Lieutenant General Hans von Zieten, the 2nd by Major General Georg von Pirch I, the 3rd by Lieutenant General Johann von Thielmann with Karl von Clausewitz as his chief of staff, and the 4th by General Count Friedrich Bülow von Dennewitz. There was one striking difference setting them off from the French and Anglo-Dutch armies : the Prussians had no cavalry reserve.

The Prussian army consisted of some 100,000 infantry divided into 136 battalions, of which 66 were *Landwehr*, 12,000 cavalry divided into 135 squadrons, of which 50 were *Landwehr*, and 39 batteries with 305 guns, mainly 6-pounders and a fcw 12-pounders.

Prussian tactics took most of their inspiration from those employed by the French.

# The French Army

Napoleon was definitely one of the most brilliant military commanders that history has ever known. His genius was not limited to conceiving battles; he was also an unrivalled organiser. While borrowing rather than inventing, he had the knack of applying other people's ideas with remarkable acuity. He had an almost photographic memory regarding terrain, human faces or the place of a text in a book, and could reduce a problem to its essentials. An egomaniac, he worked intensely and unflinchingly towards his goals. He was endowed with an unbelievable physical and mental stamina, and his intellectual audacity enabled him to take calculated risks. He saw through people and was able to exploit their weaknesses, yet he remained very much on his guard. Despite the reproaches that he directed at his lieutenants he had a certain aura of charisma, but his restless mind contributed to calling everything into doubt.

Napoleon was born in Ajaccio on the 15th August 1769, the year when James Watt patented his steam engine. His family belonged to the minor aristocracy and this origin, albeit modest, gave him access to the military academies of Brienne and Paris. It was here that he showed himself to be gifted for mathematics, history and geography. Later, as a young officer on garrison duty, he lived apart and read widely, particularly the great philosophers and military leaders. Frederick II of Prussia was his favourite. For quite some time he was carried away by an enthusiasm for the Corsican separatists, but the French Revolution gave him some unhoped-for opportunities. In 1793 his family had to leave Corsica under pressure from the counter-revolutionaries.

In December 1795 he participated in the siege of Toulon — occupied by the British at the time — as the young captain in command of the artillery. This gave him the opportunity to shine. That same month he was promoted major general — the Republic's reward to one of its few artillery officers. Thanks to

Lazare Carnot he attended a course at the Topographical Institute, where he had the opportunity to study the many plans drawn up since the time of Louis XV. In Paris he frequented those in power and was even in danger of being dragged into the Robespierre's fall. But his reputation was made when, on the 13th Vendémiaire of Year IV (5th October 1795), he saved the *Directoire* from a royalist uprising. In the meanwhile he had met the beautiful creole Joséphine Tasscher de la Pagerie, the widow of General Alexandre de Beauharnais, guillotined in 1973. Paul Barras, a member of the *Directoire,* was only too glad to be rid of his disgraced mistress. With the support of Carnot, Barras sent major general Bonaparte to Italy by way of a reward, and also to replenish the Treasury's coffers and to collect together a dowry. After a series of spectacular victories including Arcola and Rivoli, Bonaparte took it upon himself to bring negotiations with Austria to a favourable conclusion on the 17th October 1797 at Campo Formio. In addition to the creation of a pro-French cisalpine Republic, he also obtained Austria's transfer of the right bank of the Rhine to France.

The politicians feared the popularity of this general who went from success to success, and they sought a way of sidelining him. They thought that they had found a solution by giving him the command of the expeditionary force sent to Egypt to cut the British route to India. In 1798-99 he gained a series of victories, particularly at the Battle of the Pyramids. However, British naval supremacy meant that he ran the risk of being imprisoned Africa as it were, so he hurried back to France.

Napoleon seized power on the 18th and 19th Brumaire of Year VIII (9th and 10th November 1799) with the help of his brother Lucien, the President of the *Conseil des Cinq-Cents.* In a way he personified the aspirations of the bourgeoisie, which feared anarchy as much as a counter-revolution. Now that he was First Consul it was he who would govern France. It was especially after the Peace of Amiens in 1802 that he undertook the in-depth reformation of the country. He placed some of the aquisitions of the revolution on a firm footing and abolished others. In addition to founding a Central Bank he also attempted to stabilise the franc, the new monetary unit. The law was placed under secular control and codified on a centralised basis between 1804 and 1810. Emphasis was placed on individual rights, equality before the law and the right to property. Primogeniture and privilege were abolished. Napoleon also tried to reconcile the different parties and to unite them under his control.

The government's coffers were empty, however, and a second looting of Italy was called for. Napoleon defeated the second coalition in 1800 at Marengo and Hohenlinden while, at

*The walls of Hougoumont today...*

*... and as they could be seen in 1870. During the night of the 17th June they were pierced with loopholes and the farm transformed into a veritable fortress.*

the same time, continuing to work towards the edification of a rationalised and centralised French state. He regularly made sure of the support of the French people by means of plebiscites. Following upon the title of Consul for Life he became Napoleon I, Emperor of the French, in May 1804, and King of Italy in May 1805. In December 1804 he proceeded to crown himself in the presence of the Pope, whom he had managed to win over in 1801 by means of a concord between France and the Holy See.

The Emperor would create a new aristocracy based on the principle of meritocracy and would try to integrate the old nobility into it. In an economic context he showed himself to be in favour of autarky. As for the bourgeoisie, they encouraged him to adopt protectionist measures. It is true that Britain was industrially more advanced, but to maintain her economic ascendency she required free trade. From now on Albion would devote her wealth — 1,355,953,175 gold francs before the Napoleonic wars — to setting up one coalition after another to overturn France as a continental power. The political systems of the two countries were not as different as is generally claimed. It was the political systems of Prussia, Austria and Russia from which the British — and indeed the French — systems basically differed. But in name Britain was still a monarchy !

The rivalry between the two countries pushed Napoleon into preparing the invasion of Britain, who had placed herself at the head of the Third Coalition. Troops were encamped at Bologne but the French navy, badly weakened by the Revolution, did not seem to be in any condition to cover the crossing. After the defeat at Trafalgar on the 21$^{st}$ October 1805, the dream of invasion faded for good. France's naval weakness and an Austro-Russian threat explain the lightening campaigns in southern Germany and Austria. The French victories of Ulm and Austerlitz (2$^{nd}$ December 1805) dealt a mortal blow to the Third Coalition. A war against a Fourth Coalition ended in the victories of Jena and Auerstedt (14<sup>th</sup> October 1806) and eliminated Prussia as a power on the Central European stage, at least for the time being. Russia was forced to negotiate after the battles of Eylau and Friedland (1807). The Treaty of Tilsit (9<sup>th</sup> July 1807) gave Russia free rein to the east of the Niemen and in Finland. France promised assistance in the struggle against the Turks and, in exchange, the French hegemony to the west of the Niemen was recognised.

Since the weakness of the French navy did not allow a direct attack on Britain, Napoleon sought his salvation in an indirect strategy. The continental blockade, decreed against Britain since 1806, was intended to put an end to that industrialised country's prosperity and power. However, it became apparent that the blockade was a blunder in terms of grand strategy, and it in fact turned out to be a turning point in Napoleon's career. The blockade was not only ineffectual but also unpopular, especially in Denmark, the Netherlands, Italy and even in France herself — particularly in Bordeaux, Nantes and La Rochelle. The extension of the blockade to Portugal and Spain would lead to endless conflict. The Portuguese refused to apply it against their old ally Britain, and a small Anglo-Portuguese army had been supporting the Spanish insurrection since 1808. Otherwise, Britain found new outlets on the South American market.

Napoleon's absence gave fresh courage to the plotters in Paris and Vienna and a Fifth Coalition saw the light of day. In a lightening campaign Napoleon punished Austria on the 5<sup>th</sup> and 6<sup>th</sup> July 1809 at Wagram. The Emperor of Austria was only too happy when, in his search for respectability and an heir, Napoleon asked for his daughter's hand. After the Church's annulment of his childless marriage to Joséphine, Napoleon married Marie-Louise on the 10<sup>th</sup> April 1801. Expiation was complete.

In 1810 the Empire extended to Hamburg, Trieste, Rome and Barcelona. Napoleon's family — his brothers and sisters

Joseph, Louis, Elisa, Pauline, Caroline and Jérôme — reigned in Spain, the Netherlands, Tuscany, Guastalla, Naples and Westphalia. But France had aroused a ubiquitous nationalism that would gnaw away at the Empire.The absorption of the Papal States culminated in the Emperor's excommunication in 1811. His initiative set rural France — still largely catholic — against him.

*The village of Ligny, the scene of a furious infantry engagement on the 16th June (MRA collection).*

Goods from Britain continued to reach the continent, with Russia serving as a major point of entry. It was this that prompted Napoleon to set off on his march to the east. In June 1812 he embarked on a campaign with an army of some 700,000 men, only a third of whom were French. Following the battle of Borodino he entered Moscow on the 14th September 1812. The burning of the city and enormous supply problems forced him to undertake a winter retreat. Some 500,000 men did not survive and the whole of the cavalry was lost. First of all Prussia, and then Austria, abandoned the French and joined the

51

Sixth Coalition. Even Sweden, who had the French ex-marshal Charles-Jean Bernadotte in her service, turned against Napoleon. His defeat at Leipzig on the 16th-19th October 1813 at the Battle of the Nations caused France to lose control of all the territories to the east of the Rhine. In November the Austrian statesman Klemens von Metternich offered to make peace on condtion that France confined herself within the natural frontier formed by the Rhine, but Napoleon refused. During this time a revolt had broken out in the Netherlands, but Belgium remained calm. Despite the merciless conscription imperial policy had succeeded in riveting the country's attention. In January 1814 Naples abandoned the Emperor, a decision due less to Napoleon's brother-in-law Joachim Murat than to the urging of his sister Caroline. In 1814 the armies of the coalition entered France. At the head of a small army of 60,000 men Napoleon carried out a series of brilliant manoeuvres along internal axes of movement. In March he was offered a return to the frontiers of 1792, but again he refused. The final straw came after the surrender of Paris on the 31st March when his own marshals — who owed him everything — forced to him abdicate in favour of his three-year old son, the King of Rome, A few days later the allies recalled Louis XVIII from exile.

*The bridge in Genappe, towards which the remains of the Grande Armée fled on the evening of the 18th June pursued by the Prussian cavalry (Lithograph by an unknown artist, MRA collection).*

Napoleon was 46 when he returned from Elba, but his health was no longer what it had been. He was no doubt already suffering from the illness that would carry him off six years later. He no longer had the physical stamina to be everywhere and to see and correct everything. He required time, and in the morning, his troops had not always received their orders. For the first time a certain lack of decision was discernible. His strategy remained essentially offensive, however, and on the battlefield he seemed more than ever convinced of the maxim that "wars are like sieges. Fire must be concentrated on a single point. Once a breach has been made and the equilibrium destroyed, all else is vain".[5]

Napoleon was aware that France was tired of war and wanted peace. A military victory followed by a peace treaty relatively favourable to France was his only defence against political disaster. The army had both its strong points and its weaknesses. It was made up of veterans, including ex-prisoners back from Russia, Germany and Britain, all of whom had had the experience of at least one campaign. There were no longer any unreliable allies as there had been in the past. Even so, a certain animosity still reigned in the ranks between those who had remained faithful to Napoleon after his abdication and those who had worn the white cockade. The former feared treason, particularly in the case of the generals, while the latter laughed at the old campaigners. It is open to question whether certain of the generals really believed in the adventure. But, quite apart from the quarrel between the Bourbons and the Bonapartists, the territorial integrity of France was also at stake. All those with a "de" in their names were suspect. Didn't Napoleon himself once remark "once a white, always a white"?

The chief of staff appointed by Napoleon was the 46-year old Nicholas Jean de Dieu Soult, the Duke of Dalmatia, the son of a notary and the eternal loser in Spain. It was an odd choice. A short time previously Soult had been Louis XVIII's Minister of War, a post in which he had made a great deal of being a

---

5. J. VIAL, *Histoire abrégée des campagnes modernes*, Vol. I, Paris, 1910, p. 14.

staunch royalist. His orders often lacked clarity and arrived late. He did not seem to be cut out to be the intellectual that Marshal Alexandre Berthier was. However, he did have the services of Berthier's outstanding deputy in the person of Comte François Bailly de Monthion. A large number of generals, including Dominique Vandamme and Jean-Baptiste Drouet d'Erlon, contested Soult's authority. The appointment as cavalry commander of the Marquis Emmanuel de Grouchy, a brilliant horseman and a recently promoted marshal, was no doubt a judicious move. Upon entering Belgium Napoleon entrusted him with the right wing of his army and, subsequently, with the pursuit of the Prussians after Ligny. There can be no doubt that his appointment as the commander of a large force operating virtually independently and his promotion to marshal were dictated by the need to win the old aristocracy to the regime. Even stranger was the choice of Marshal Michel Ney, also aged 46, to command the left wing and, later, to lead the attacks to force a breakthrough at Waterloo. Ney was not particularly phlegmatic or bright. In the past he had always referred to A. de Jomini, his Swiss chief of staff. But the soldiers and the junior ranks thought highly of the Prince of the Moskova. And his appointment did demonstrate that Napoleon was capable of forgiving those who had abandoned him in 1814. It is true that while these different appointments might come as as a surprise, Napoleon hardly had any choice. Only five of the 28 imperial Marshals were still in his service in 1815.

The corps commanders were all widely experienced. Drouet d'Erlon, who had been imprisoned during the restoration, received the command of the 1st corps. Honoré Reille was entrusted with the 2nd. Dominique Vandamme, a Frenchman from the north (Cassel) and the son of a surgeon from Moorslede, received the 3rd, Etienne Gérard the 4th and Georges Mouton, Comte de Lobau, the 6th. The cavalry was divided into four smaller corps of two divisions each. The 1st corps was placed under the command of Claude Pujol, the 2nd went to General Remi Exelmans from the frontier town of Bar-le-Duc, the 3rd to François Kellerman, the son of the marshal, and the 4th to Jean Baptiste Milhaud. The Imperial

Guard, consisting of infantry, cavalry and artillery, was placed under Antoine Drouot. The wole army had some 160 generals and a staff of about 600. For political reasons Napoleon accepted onto his staff a certain number of young people — idealists for the most part — who often failed in their appointed duty of carrying despatches.

Equipping the army caused enormous problems that were caused mainly by delays on the part of the suppliers. Their lack of enthusiasm can be understood given that earlier bills had frequently never been paid. Neither Napoleon nor his War Minister Davout nor, indeed, the ever-present Lazare Carnot could really afford to take drastic action for reasons of public order.

The infantry, 90,600 strong and divided into 174 batallions, was excellent. A company contained a hundred or so men, and six companies formed a batallion of 500-600 men. Two batallions formed a regiment, two regiments a brigade and two brigades a division. A division thus contained some 5,000 men plus a six-gun battery, two mortars, an engineer company and a supply train. The infantry's armament left a lot to be desired. Apart from the *model 1777* musket there were arms acquired illegally in Britain or bought from the peasants at twelve francs apiece. In the matter of uniforms confusion reigned supreme. Not all the grenadiers had fur caps and there were too few shakos. The brass plates with the Bourbon coat of arms that had adorned the headdress had either been removed, or had been beaten flat and filled in with a hurriedly engraved eagle. Everybody wore a tricolour cockade. A piece of knotted cloth generally did service as a knapsack, and the musket was often carried with the help of a length of rope.

The cavalry — 22,300 men in 170 squadrons — was no longer as impetuous as in the days of glory. More than one cuirassier had no cuirasse. The quality of the horses also left a lot to be desired, to say nothing of their supplies. There were too few scythes to cut hay. A cavalry division had 1,500 men, and its organisation was the same as that of an infantry division

*Following pages :*
*The centre of the*
*British army in action.*
*An artist's impression*
*(Lithograph by*
*T. Sutherland after*
*W. Heath. MRA*
*collection)*

except that a regiment consisted of three or four squadrons of 120-200 sabres each. The attached artillery was mounted and equipped with four guns and two mortars.

The French artillery had 6,000 men and 47 batteries, i.e. 372 guns — 6- and 12-pounders and 6-inch mortars. It was considered to be the best in the matter of speed and accuracy.

The engineers had 1,500 well-trained men.

The medical and supply services operated at army corps level. The bridging equipment was controlled by Napoleon's staff, as were the artillery and engineer reserves.

# CHAPTER IV

# Napoleon's manoeuvres

Prince William of Orange's 1$^{st}$ corps was deployed at Nivelles and Soignies and in the vicinity of Enghien. The dispersal area of Hill's 2$^{nd}$ corps was much greater, extending as it did to Ghent, Oudenaarde, Ath, Mons, Tournai, Menin and Ypres. Uxbridge's cavalry was stationed in the Zottegem-Ninove area while Wellington's headquarters and reserves were in Brussels and the immediate vicinity. Antwerp and Ostend — two key positions on the line of communication — were heavily guarded, as were Brussels and Ghent, where Louis XVIII had taken refuge with his court. The front was 80 kms broad and 50 deep. Wellington envisaged three possible axes along which the French might attack, namely between the Lys and the Scheldt, along the banks of the Scheldt, or between the Scheldt and the Sambre. He anticipated giving battle in the Halle-Nivelles-Enghien area and counted heavily on the Prussians coming to his aid on his left flank. The two armies had liaison officers in attendance.

Zieten's 1$^{st}$ Prussian corps was encamped around Charleroi, Pirch I's 2$^{nd}$ extended from Wavre to Huy via Namur and Thielmann's 3$^{rd}$ was in the vicinity of Ciney. As for the 4$^{th}$

(Bülow), its dispersal area was larger and took in Liège and Maastricht. Blücher had his headquarters in Namur. The Prussian army controlled the Sambre and Meuse valleys and the line of communication to the Rhine. Their dispositions were 60 kms broad and 50 kms deep. Like Wellington, at the beginning of June Blücher still did not believe that Napoleon would attack. A concentric invasion of France was set to begin on the 1st July.

Thanks to his agents and to various newspapers, especially the *Gazette de Bâle,* Napoleon was well aware of was being hatched against him. He therefore decided to attack. To ensure his freedom of action and to make the most of the means at his disposal he made every effort to mislead his opponents and to surprise them. His preparations were carried out in secret and, on the 3rd June the order was given to increase the surveillance of the frontiers, to break off all communications with abroad, to intercept the mail, to block the roads, to construct strongpoints and to restore town fortifications, etc. On the 10th June 1815 the Emperor was in his box at the Théâtre Français for a performance of *Hector*. The following day — a Sunday — he attended mass. On the 12th June he stayed secretly in Laon and on the 13th he issued his orders from Avesnes. The National Guard — a sort of local defence force — simulated a series of

*Uniforms.*
**From left to right :**
*A British corporal of the 27th (Inniskilling) Regiment of Foot.*
*A lieutenant of a rifle company of the Dutch Regiment of Nassau,*
*A trooper of the British 18th Hussars.*

manoeuvres in the Lille area. Was the Lys — the traditional invasion route — going to be used after all? What would the Duke of Wellington do? Beat a hasty retreat towards the coast?

During this time Napoleon decided to concentrate the Northern Army in the vicinity of Beaumont and Philippeville, which were still French at the time. From there he would drive back the Prussians at Charleroi and cross the Sambre. While he was attacking and defeating the Prussians, a shadowing force would keep the British at arm's length. He would then be able to turn upon the Anglo-Dutch forces. Without placing too much faith in the idea he hoped that the British would accept battle, but he was afraid that they would retreat in the direction of Ostend and Antwerp. As for the Belgians, Napoleon thought that after the fall of Brussels they would come out in favour of his cause. This plan was thus one of manoeuvering along internal axes, but on a reduced scale.

The Emperor had, however, also planned another manoeuvre of the same type, but on a much larger scale. After his victory in the Netherlands he would leave a small shadowing force there and, with the bulk of his army, would join Rapp to meet the Austrians and the Russians. Once again, he would carry out a small-scale manoeuvre along internal axes

*A musketeer of the 1st Pomeranian Regiment. A lieutenant colonel of the Dutch Light Dragoons A gunner, British Foot Artillery, 1815 (MRA collecltion).*

of movement. Napoleon hoped that the successes obtained in this way would bring him further support in France and would cause the Seventh Coalition to collapse. In order to be able to carry out all these manoeuvres his soldiers would have to march longer and more rapidly than their opponents.

Napoleon's troops were organised as follows. Behind a screen of a dozen cavalry regiments the army was split into three major axes of advance. The left wing was made up of the 2nd corps (Reille) followed by the 1st (Drouet d'Erlon). This wing was to march from Soltre-sur-Sambre towards Leers on the frontier, and then towards Thuin and Marchienne-au-Pont. In the centre the 1st cavalry corps (Pajol) was in the van, followed by the 3rd corps (Vandamme), the bridging equipment, the Guard and the 6th corps (Lobau). Setting out from Beaumont, these troops were to cross the frontier at Strée and advance on Marcinelle and Charleroi. The right-hand column consisted of the 4th corps (Gérard), reinforced by a cavalry division. After leaving Philippeville this column was to march in the direction of Florennes, on the frontier, in order to reach Charleroi, where it would cross the Sambre. As for the cavalry reserve under Grouchy, it too was to move on Charleroi once it had crossed the frontier at Tingremont.

These dispositions initially extended over a 35-kilometre front, but once the Sambre had been crossed the front was reduced to some 10 kilometres. The larger the column, the longer it took to pass — about four hours for the 40,000 strong left-hand column; about six for the main body — more than 60,000 men — in the centre, and fewer than two for the right-hand column with slightly more than 15,000 men. These forces could be grouped together in six hours, which was in fact the minimum duration of a battle.

The light cavalry — responsible for reconnaissance — mounted up at 2.30 am on the 15th June after the sounding of the *Diane*. Most of the infantry set off at about three, and the last cavalry moved out towards half past five. After a march of some

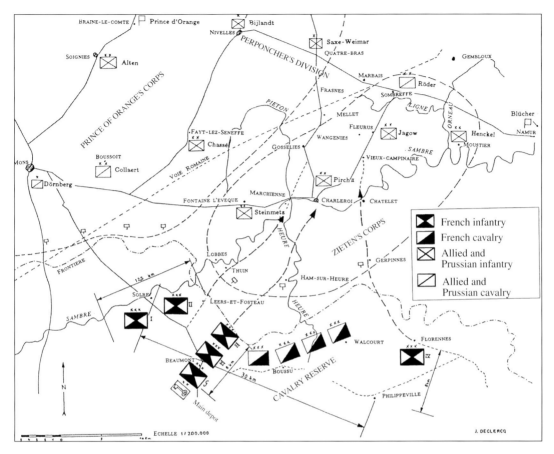

Map legend:

- French infantry
- French cavalry
- Allied and Prussian infantry
- Allied and Prussian cavalry

ECHELLE 1/200.000

J. DECLERCQ

30 kms, the bulk of the forces was to be across the Sambre by midday.

It is probable that the initial objective was the Quatre-Bras, Sombreffe and Fleurus triangle. This would make it possible to group the army and to ensure the control of the Charleroi-Brussels, the Charleroi-Sombreffe and the Nivelles-Namur roads as well as the old Roman road, popularly known as the *Chaussée Brunehaut,* that followed the watershed between the Scheldt and the Meuse basins. This road was a convenient link between France and Germany, and the region that it crosses has been the scene of numerous battles including those of Gembloux (1578 & 1940), Fleurus (1662, 1690 & 1794), Neerwinden (1693 & 1793), Ramilles (1706), Malplaquet (1709) and Mons and Charleroi (1914).

*The positions of the troops on the 14th June before nightfall, and the French advance on the 15th.*

Did Napoleon think that Dutch was spoken everywhere in Belgium? In his movement orders of 14th June he stated "Reille, Vandamme, Gérard and Pajol (...) will, as far as possible, have Flemish-speaking officers in the advance guard to question the inhabitants and obtain intelligence"!

In his proclamation of the 14th June the Emperor sought to inspire his troops with courage. After recalling that it was the anniversary of Marengo and Friedland he went on to speak of Austerlitz and Wagram and asked: "Surely we are the same men as they were?" And he finished by evoking the dissatisfaction of six million (sic) Belgians, absorbed into a new Kingdom and forced to fight for princes hostile to justice and people's rights.

In the meanwhile Brussels was making the most of the presence of a great number of British who paid cash, played with the children and caroused. The ball that the Duke and Duchess of Richmond were giving was "the" subject of converation in polite society. Two hundred and forty invitations were sent out that included all the generals, and some ADCs and staff officers among others. The Duke of Richmond, the future governor of Canada, had beeen renting a town house in the Rue de la Blanchisserie (today Nos 106-114, Rue des Marais) since July 1814. Together with his wife he gave a British flavour to Brussels society. People were delighted to be able to attend the grand military ceremony planned for the 21st July to mark the Battle of Vittoria, at which Wellington had defeated Marshal Jourdan in 1813.

During this time the Dutch and Prussians were standing by. On the 14th June General van Merlen, who commanded a cavalry brigade in the vicinity of Binche, reported the approach of the French. Peasants could be seen fleeing with their carts and their animals. On the same day Wilhelm von Dörnberg, a Prussian cavalry general, announced that some 100,000 French had assembled in the Philippeville area and that the units facing him on the frontier had disappeared. In the night of the 14th June

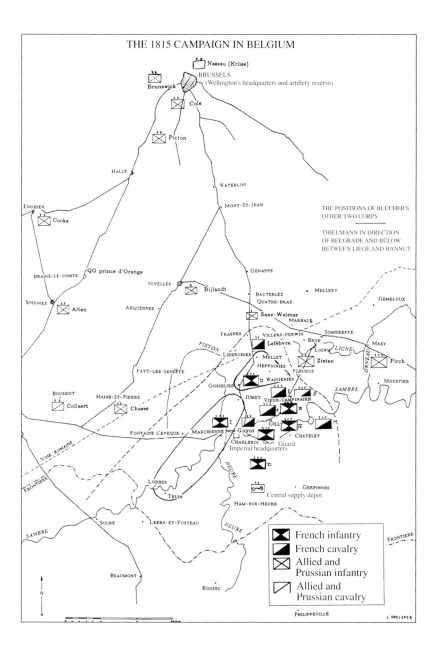

THE 1815 CAMPAIGN IN BELGIUM

Nassau (Krüse)

BRUSSELS
(Wellington's headquarters and artillery reserve)

Brunswick

Cole

Picton

HALLE

WATERLOO

MONT-ST-JEAN

THE POSITIONS OF BLÜCHER'S
OTHER TWO CORPS

THIELMANN IN DIRECTION
OF BELGRADE AND BÜLOW
BETWEEN LIÈGE AND HANNUT

ENGHIEN

Cocke

QG prince d'Orange

GENAPPE

BRAINE-LE-COMTE

NIVELLES

Bijlandt

MELLERY

SOIGNIES

Alten

ARQUENNES

BAUTERLEZ
QUATRE-BRAS.

GEMBLOUX

Saxe-Weimar
MARBAIS

SOMBREFFE

FRASNES

VILLERS-PERWIN

BRYE

MAZY

Lefebvre

LIGNY LIGNE

PIETON

LIBERCHIES

MELLET

LIGNY

Zieten

Pirch

HEPPIGNIES

FLEURUS

FAYT-LEZ-SENEFFE

Wangenies

GOSSELIES

SAMBRE

MOUSTIER

BOUSSOIT

HAINE-ST-PIERRE

Collaert

Chassé

JUMET

VIEUX-CAMPINAIRE

FONTAINE L'EVEQUE

MARCHIENNE

Guyot

GILLY

CHATELET

CHARLEROI

Guard
Imperial headquarters

VOIE ROMAINE

HEURE

FRONTIERE

LOBBES

GERPINNES

THUIN

Central supply depot

HAM-SUR-HEURE

SAMBRE

SOLRE

LEERS-ET-FOSTEAU

HEURE

FRONTIERE

BEAUMONT

N

BOUSSU

French infantry
French cavalry
Allied and
Prussian infantry
Allied and
Prussian cavalry

PHILIPPEVILLE

J. DECLERCQ

Blücher gave Zieten the order to undertake delaying operations between the frontier and Fleurus while the main body of troops was concentrating in the Sombreffe area.

# CHAPTER V

# 15th June:
# The French advance

The Emperor spent his last night on what was still French soil at Beaumont, where he stayed in the Château of the Princes of Caraman Chimay. As for the French army, its bivouacs were spread out over an area 35 kms. by 9.

Various instances of careless staff work and delays in passing on orders held up departure from two in the morning to four, and some units were completely intermingled. Once in Belgium, the army wasted time looting and looking for food. Progress was very difficult because of the unmade roads, the forests and the steep valleys. The guns sank in up to their axles.

After a few brief exchanges the advance guard of the left-hand column crossed the Sambre towards 1 pm. However, having obtained the agreement of Hendrik Perponcher-Sedlnitzky, his divisional commander, de Constant-Rebecque, the chief of staff of the 1$^{st}$ Dutch corps, sent Saxe-Weimar's brigade of 4,300 men to the important Quatre-Bras crossroads to ensure its safety. Bijland's brigde was despatched to Nivelles in support.

At four in the afternoon Napoleon belatedly summoned Ney — the latter had changed sides several times! — and entrusted him with the command of the left wing, i.e. the 1$^{st}$ and 2$^{nd}$ corps and a Guards cavalry division. After taking Gosselies Ney came up against a Nassau batallion and a Dutch battery. Deploying for the attack took a certain amount of time, but the allies were repulsed towards half past six. A little after 7.30 a skirmish took place 2 kms to the south of Quatre-Bras, but Ney did not insist because he thought that he was ahead of the other columns. That evening the troops of his left wing were spread out beween Jumet and Thuin; the concentration of his forces had failed. Ney spent the evening at Gosselies in the house of Melchior Dumon, an industrialist living in the Rue Saint-Roch. After punishing the burgundy he no doubt slept like a log !

Progress in the centre and on the right was slowed down largely because of the state of the ground, which was sodden after weeks of rain. During the night of the 14$^{th}$ June General Count Victor de Bourmont, the commander of the 14$^{th}$ divison of the 4$^{th}$ corps, deserted with some of his staff — a circumstance which did not exactly help things along. In his farewell letter to General Gérard he wrote, "I am unable to fight for a government which has proscribed my parents and almost all of the landowners in my province". In reading these lines one can imagine the feelings of their author, torn between the defence of the interests of France and those of the Napoleonic regime which represented her at the time.

Towards midday the centre column reached Charleroi, and the engineers and marines set about destroying the palisade protecting the bridge. Supported by the Guards, Pajol's cavalry were then able to occupy the town, which had been abandoned by the Prussians. When he arrived Napoleon was applauded by the local liberals and as well as by his own troops.

Because of the confusion and the low capacity of the Charleroi Bridge Napoleon ordered Gérard to cross the Sambre with the right-hand column by the bridge at Châtelet. But

Prussian troops, hidden in the woods on the Soleilmont Abbey heights, controlled the eastern access to Châtelet and Charleroi. Since the cavalry was unable to dislodge them Grouchy decided to send in Vandamme's infantry, but the latter refused to obey, claiming that a verbal order from Napoleon was insufficient to appoint Grouchy to command the right wing, and so the 3rd and 4th corps and the cavalry.

At about half past six that evening Napoleon took command of the right wing in person, and towards seven Pirch I's Prussians withdrew in the direction of Lambusart and Fleurus. In the meantime night had fallen. The French troops, who had marched between 30 and 40 kms in stifling heat, were roaming about looking for something to eat before sinking into a deep sleep. As for Napoleon, he quartered himself in the *basse ville* of Charleroi, in the house of the ironmaster Puissant (19, Rue Léopold, today the site of the local branch of the National Bank), where he had already lunched at the table occupied by... Zieten at breakfast ! He went to bed shortly after

*Marshal Ney, the* **Bravest of the Brave,** *or* **Old Redhead.** *As he predicted, he ended up in front of an émigré firing squad. (After Perboyre, MRA collection).*

nine. The report that his lieutenants sent to Paris was a model of exaggeration.

Meanwhile, at six that evening General F. von Müffling, the Prussian liaison officer at Wellington's headquarters, handed the Duke a message from Gneisenau. He informed Wellington that the French attack was not a diversionary manoeuvre and that Blücher was going to concentrate his troops in the vicinity of Sombreffe. An hour later Wellington issued a movement order which he modified towards 11 pm. While ordering part of his forces to concentrate in the vicinity of Nivelles, he had other troops cover his line of communication to Ostend. Whereas his first order meant a movement towards the south-west, the second clearly indicated one in a north easterly direction.

At eleven that evening the Duke attended a soirée at the Duke and Duchess of Richmond's. All Brussels was present.

The Prince de Ligne, the Dukes of Arenberg, the Comte d'Oultremont, the Comte de Mercy d'Argenteau and the Marquis d'Assche mixed with the British aristocracy, the Princes of Orange and a number of ADCs, including a certain C. H. Churchill.

At 11.30 pm a dust-covered lieutenant Henry Webster brought a message from de Constant-Rebecque. The officer had ridden on horseback from Braine-le-Comte to Brussels — some 30 kms — in the record time of one hour forty minutes. In his letter the chief of staff of the Dutch forces announced that the French had arrived in front of Quatre-Bras. Wellington decided to speed up the concentration of his forces. Those attending the soirée did not really know what was happening, but once the situation was known, calm returned. With his usual phlegm Wellington indicated that he had no further orders to give and thereby restored the mood of the evening.

However, towards one in the morning the Duke discreetly ordered his officers to leave. He himself slipped away towards three. He confirmed his Dutch lieutenants' decisions and ordered the concentration of the bulk of his army at Quatre-Bras. After a few hours' rest he mounted his horse seven in the morning of the 16<sup>th</sup> and galloped off in the direction of Quatre-Bras.The first British units had left Brussels by the Porte de Halle two hours previously.

*The Emperor's final headquarters. The farm of Le Caillou was burnt on the morning of the 19th June (Lithograph by an unknown artist, MRA collection).*

71

In the meantime de Constant-Rebecque had set up his headquarters at Quatre-Bras, where the Prince of Orange arrived at about five in the morning. At nine he had barely 4,300 men and eight guns at Quatre-Bras, but by two in the afternoon the number had risen to 7,500 men and 16 guns. Facing him, more than 13,000 men and 24 guns were awaiting the order to attack.

On St. Helena Napoleon admitted that de Constant-Rebecque's decision to deploy troops to Quatre-Bras was the move which prevented him from catching the British out. It was this stroke of genius — initially attributed by Napoleon to the Prince of Orange — which was largely responsible for the final outcome of the 1815 campaign. And nobody seems to have thought otherwise! After the battle the Prince was granted a palace in Brussels as a token of gratitude. This is the present Palais des Académies. And he was given an estate at Tervueren so that he could build a second home. This would become the Colonial Museum — today the Central African Museum.

# CHAPTER VI

# 16th June : The two battles

Napoleon most certainly did not work during the night of the 15th June. He had received different reports which enabled him to obtain an idea of the situation, and in the morning he got his thinking straight. He believed that the Prussians would retire on Maastricht. He would take advantage of this to come to Ney's aid and, together, they would march on Brussels. The British would doubtlessly retire towards the coast. The Emperor formalised these different ideas in two orders which were despatched to Ney and Grouchy. He confirmed the division of his army into two parts of some 40,000 to 50,000 men each under the command of Ney and Grouchy respectively. He himself assumed command of the reserve, consisting of the Guard. He issued the directives required to avoid any problems of authority. He would come to the assistance of one wing or the other, as circumstances demanded. If the need arose, he would weaken one wing to reinforce the reserve. He would exercise direct command over the army corps from where he was. He informed Grouchy that he would arrive at Fleurus between 10 and 11 am and would fight if the Prussians resisted. He put their strength at 40,000 men. And, lastly, he ordered Ney to occupy Quatre-Bras.

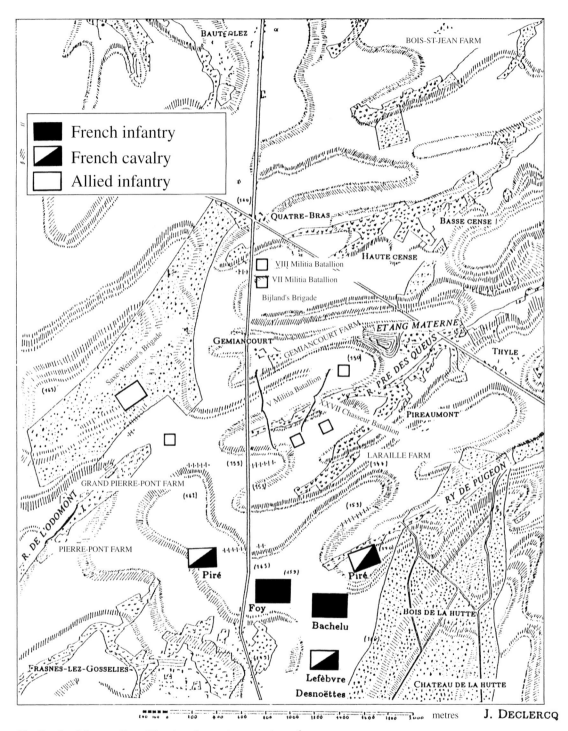

*The Battle of Quatre-Bras. The situation at 2 pm on the 16th June.*

At half past nine Napoleon learnt that a large body of troops was marching towards Quatre-Bras. At this he sent a second order to Ney telling him to engage the troops arriving from Brussels.

It was almost eleven when Ney received the first order. From this he learnt that Napoleon would attack at about three in the afternoon or in the evening, and that he might require some of his units. In the meantime C. Lefèbvre-Desnouettes' cavalry division was to rejoin the Guard, and Kellerman's cavalry corps would take its place.

The French troops had not succeeded in regrouping during the morning and were spread out over an area more than 25 kilometres in depth. And it took quite some time for orders to arrive in units further down the chain of command.

Blücher intended to fight, possibly at Sombreffe, with only three corps. Wellington arrived at Quatre-Bras towards half past nine. A worrying calm reigned. What were Napoleon's intentions? At 12.45 Blücher and Wellington met at Bussy mill in the neighbourhood of Brye.

At quarter to eleven Grouchy learnt that he had been confirmed in his appointment as commander of the right wing. Shortly afterwards Napoleon appeared on the field and could see for himself that the Prussians were deploying for battle. Blücher had placed Zieten's 1$^{st}$ corps behind the Grand Ry and the Ligne, two small marshy rivers some 3-4 metres wide, and he positioned Pirch's 2$^{nd}$ corps in the second echelon. These manoeuvres took place in perfect order because the Prussians had reconnoitred the terrain two months earlier.

Napoleon realised that only a regular battle could drive the Prussians back. He therefore ordered his right wing to regroup, but this meant further marching that devolved mainly on Gérard's 4$^{th}$ Corps and the Guard. After installing himself in the Naveau mill he personally wrote out an order to Ney at 1 pm instructing him to attack and occupy Quatre-Bras. He hoped that Ney would then be in a position to move along the Namur road and carry out a flank attack on the Prussians. But this order did not reach Ney until late in the afternoon, just before five.

Around two o'clock Napoleon had some 70,000 men and 242 guns at his disposal. But around three Blücher succeeded in extending his line to the left by deploying Thielmann's 3$^{rd}$ corps between Sombreffe and Mazy. Blücher thus had 83,000 men and 224 guns, but he waited for the arrival of his 4$^{th}$ Corps before making any move.

At about half past two Napoleon was ready for battle, but half an hour earlier the battle of Quatre-Bras had already begun barely 12 kms away.

## The Battle of Quatre-Bras

Ney had been waiting impatiently since morning for orders that did not arrive. At seven o'clock he had set out to reconnoitre Frasnes and spotted Saxe-Weimar's men. They were probably outposts. Ney was worried about the Prussians' movements and nervous about his right flank. Wouldn't the occupation of Quatre-Bras make it more vulnerable to Prussian attack ? What were his commander's intentions ?

Napoleon's instructions finally arrived at about eleven o'clock. Ney rapidly issued his orders: those units of Reille's 2$^{nd}$ corps that were present were placed in position - Gilbert Bachelu's division on the extreme right, opposite Pireaumont farm, and Maximilien Foy's astride the Charleroi-Quatre-Bras road. The cavalry was ready to engage wherever necessary. All in all Ney had more than 13,000 men and 24 guns. With the arrival of Bijland's brigade William of Orange could count on more than 7,500 men and 16 guns.

The battlefield, which formed a triangle approximately 3 kms from top to bottom and the same across its base, was covered with almost ripe rye. The French units were deployed behind a small ridge some 2,500 metres to the south of Quatre-Bras. Hills 162, 165 and 166 were hardly noticeable against the background of the slightly sloping terrain. Yet these three hills marked the watershed between the Meuse basin with the Ruisseau d'Odomont stream, and the Scheldt basis with, amongst others, the Gémioncourt, the Le Pré des Queues and the Ry du Pigeon streams. The battlefield was limited to the west by the Bois de Bossu wood, which no longer exists, and to the south-east by the Bois de la Hutte.

Ney ordered the attack to be sounded at two in the afternoon. Bachelu was able to seize Pireaumont farm with the support of his divisional artillery and 16 guns posted along the ridge. A counter-attack by the 5th Militia Battalion under Prince William was attacked in the flank by the cavalry. Foy drove the Dutch from the mighty Gémioncourt farm, but his left-hand

*"They were giants on enormous horses" — Cuirassiers charging British squares (MRA collection)*

brigade failed at Grand Pierrepont. At three o'clock the division under Jèrôme, Napoleon's youngest brother, arrived on the field with more than 7,000 men. They set about capturing Grand Pierrepont farm and drove the Nassau troops into the Bois de Bossu wood.

At four o'clock van Merlen's light cavalry brigade (1,100 men) arrived to reinforce the allies and covered the deployment of Picton's 5th Division (7,700 men). Two brigades formed squares some 400 metres to the south of the crossroads while the 3rd brigade established itself in the shelter of the embankment along the Namur road. There was a moment of confusion when the British opened fire on Van Merlen's

*La Papelotte farm in 1815. Devastated by the fighting, it was restored in 1860.*

*It was then that the bell-turret was added which surmounts it today (Lithograph by Sturm, MRA collection).*

Belgian dragoons, whose uniforms were similar to those of the French *chasseurs*. This unit — the 5$^{th}$ Light Dragoons — formed the nucleus of the future Belgian 1$^{st}$ Lancers. Durng this time a 3,800 strong Brunswick brigade was locked in battle with Jérôme's division.

At about half past four Napoleon learnt via an intermediary from the 6$^{th}$ Corps that Ney was engaged in a regular battle, and this was confirmed by the noise of cannon-fire that he could hear. It was about this time that Ney received Napoleon's one o'clock message to attack and capture Quatre-Bras.

In the meanwhile Bachelu's division was working its way towards the Namur road. His horse artillery opened up at short range on the British squares. As for Jérôme's infantry, it was forcing its way through the Bois de Bossu wood. But the Brunswick infantry fought with a total disregard for death. The Death's Head Hussars launched an attack on the outskirts of the wood, but Hippolyte Piré's numerically much stronger cavalry intervened and the Brunswick units were driven off. As he was endeavouring to halt the retreat Duke Frederick William of Brunswick was killed at the spot where a commemorative monument now stands. Returning from his meeting with Blücher, Wellington narrowly avoided disaster thanks to his excellent horse *Copenhagen* and the square formed by the 92$^{nd}$ Highlanders.

While this was going on Ney received further orders from Napoleon, this time requesting him to intervene on the Prussians' right flank. Meeting the 1$^{st}$ corps along the way La Bédoyère, the Emperor's ADC, ordered them not to join Ney but to march towards Napoleon.

The orders and counter-orders and the clear instruction received at eleven o'clock that morning prompted Ney to recall the 1$^{st}$ corps. After all, hadn't Napoleon been quite unam-biguous in placing it under his command ? How could he go to the Emperor's aid when he had a resolute enemy opposing him ?

Towards half past five von Alten's division arrived. This meant that there were now more Anglo-Dutch than French in the field.

At about the same time Ney discovered from the duplicate of an order from Napoleon that the Emperor was waiting impatiently for his support. Ney therefore ordered Kellermann to carry out a series of charges. The 69th Foot lost their colours, but a battery of the King's German Legion was able to save the situation. The cuirassiers fled, and Kellermann only just escaped capture. Faced with this failure Ney launched himself into a number of charges agains the enemy, losing several horses shot beneath him in the process.

The arrival of the British Guards towards half past six finally tipped the balance in Wellington's favour. He was now fighting with 35,000 men and 70 guns against barely 23,000 French supported by 24 guns. The three farms were recaputured by Wellington's troops. Nightfall saved the French, and fighting ceased about nine. During this time d'Erlon's men were still marching between the two wings.

The French lost 4,375 men and the Anglo-Dutch 4,650. Wellington had succeeded in concentrating his troops and Quatre-Bras remained in the allies' hands.

## The Battle of Ligny

It was terribly hot at half past two that afternoon and Napoleon and his Guard were still at the Naveau mill, not far from Fleurus. Vandamme's 3rd corps was deployed on his left, near Saint-Amand. In the centre, Gérard's 4th corps was near Ligny. Operating under Grouchy's orders, Exelman's and Pujol's cavalry covered the right flank while Jean Domon's cavalry division protected the left.

The Ligny battlefield extends over a slightly undulating plateau crossed by a small river — the Ligne — and the Grand Ry that flows into it. At Bâlatre, to the east of the battlefield, the Ligne is about 4 metres wide. The valley is marshy in a number of places, and at one point falls steeply away. From Fleurus the land slopes downwards in a northerly direction and then rises beyond the rivers. The Bussy mill, where Blücher had set up his observation post, was on the top of hill 162 and dominated the surrounding countryside.

The Prussians had fortified themselves in a dozen villages and hamlets extending some 9 kms along the Ligne and the winding Grand-Ry. The houses were mostly built of strong local stone. There were scarcely any trees except round the villages and in the valleys. The fields were covered with different kinds of cereals.

*The fighting at Hougoumont farm — an artist's impression (Lithograph by Jobard after Madou, MRA collection).*

In the early stages Napoleon wanted to use Grouchy's cavalry (12,000 men) to shadow Thielemann's corps (23,000

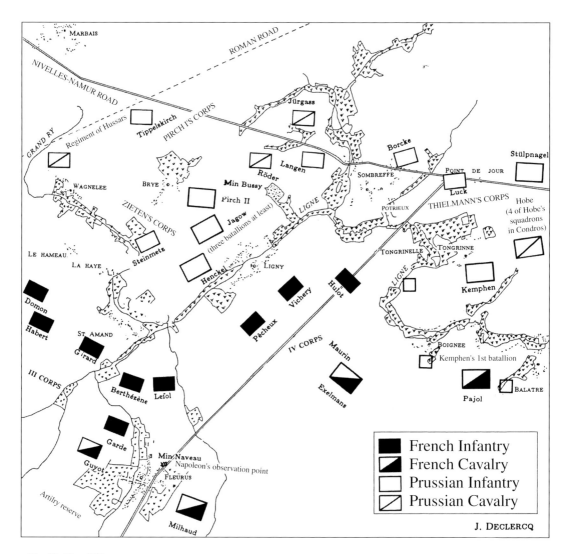

MARBAIS

ROMAN ROAD

NIVELLES-NAMUR ROAD

GRAND RY

Regiment of Hussars

Tippelskirch

PIRCH I'S CORPS

Jürgass

Borcke

Stülpnagel

Langen

Röder

SOMBREFFE

POINT DE JOUR

WAGNELEE

BRYE

Min Bussy

Pirch II

Luck

THIELMANN'S CORPS

Hobe
(4 of Hobe's
squadrons
in Condros)

ZIETEN'S CORPS

Jagow
(three batallions at least)

LIGNE

POTRIEUX

Steinmetz

LE HAMEAU

LA HAYE

Li

TONGRINELLE

TONGRINNE

LIGNY

Henckel

Ligny

Hulot

Kemphen

Domon

Vichery

LIGNE

Habert

St. AMAND

Gérard

Péchaux

Maurin

BOIGNEE

IV CORPS

Exelmans

Kemphen's 1st batallion

III CORPS

Berthézène

Lefol

BALATRE

Pajol

Garde

Guyot

Min Naveau
Napoleon's observation point

French Infantry

French Cavalry

FLEURUS

Prussian Infantry

Prussian Cavalry

Artilry reserve

Milhaud

J. DECLERCQ

**The Battle of Ligny on the 16th June 1815. Situation at 2 pm.**

men) while he himself attacked with Gérard's and Vandamme's corps in order to pin down the Prussians in the centre. Arriving from the Namur road in the west, Ney's troops were to surprise the Prussian right flank. In this way Blücher would be definitely cut off from Wellington. Napoleon had some 66,000 men for the main thrust and was expecting reinforcements in the shape of Ney's 20,000-30,000. On the opposing side the Prussians had only 60,000.

Between half past two and three the artillery started to bombard the Prussian infantry, which was partly in the open.

Three cannon shots fired by the Guard gave the signal to attack. It was three o'clock in the afternoon. Vandamme's 3rd corps rushed in but suffered heavy losses because of the open ground. The French succeeded in taking Saint-Amand and Le Hameau. The Prussians, who were on the defensive along the Ligne, were threatened with an attack from the rear. Blücher sent them reinforcements. Girard was seriously injured falling from his horse, which had been killed outright. On 21st June he was made Duke of Ligny, but a few days later he died of his injuries.

While the first attack against Ligny failed, the second, with better artillery support, succeeded and the French were able to seize the part of the village on the eastern bank. Napoleon promptly moved part of his cavalry to the left, and Blücher followed suit to reinforce his now threatened wing.

At about four o'clock Grouchy carried out a diversionary movement in the direction of Tongrinne, and an hour later Hulot advanced in the same direction.

Towards half past five the Emperor considered that the time now was ripe since the Prussians' centre had been weakened to assist their right wing. In the meanwhile Napoleon had discovered that he could not count on Ney's support. He had the Guards and Milhaud's cavalry drawn up to break through the centre. Blücher's right flank would then be surrounded.

However, one of Vandamme's liaison officers caused a panic by reporting the arrival of an unidentified column from the Villers-Perwin direction. Napoleon broke off the deployment of the force earmarked for the breakthrough because he was afraid of having to engage his reserves to confront a new enemy. It was now six.

*Following pages: Furious fighting in the village of Ligny, 16th June 1815 (MRA collection)*

*The hazards of mounted warfare — at 72 years of age. In the evening of the battle of Ligny Blücher was knocked off his horse and only a miracle saved him from capture. (Lithograh by S. Milan after G. Jones. MRA collection).*

This pause enabled Blücher to repulse the French wing and to retake Le Hameau. The Young Guard and part of the Old Guard had to intervene to restore the situation. An attack by Thielmann on the Fleurus road caused some further confusion.

In the meanwhile the column sighted a short time before turned out to be d'Erlon's 1st corps. It had got to within 3 kms of Saint-Amand and then, recalled by Ney, had marched away again.

It was now seven o'clock. It was starting to rain, and a storm was brewing. Napoloeon placed himself at the head of the greater part of his Guard and various reserve troops. The cavalry protected the flanks. The artillery concentrated its fire on Ligny and 20,000 men launched themselves through the village in the direction of Brye. It was now half past eight.

Placing himself at the head of some cavalry, Blücher tried to halt the French advance. The septuagenarian field marshal's grey horse, a magnificent animal that had been presented to him by Britain's Prince Regent, was killed, and he experienced a nasty fall. He owed his salvation to the darkness because there were cuirassiers everywhere. Covered by their cavalry and under Gneisenau's skilful leadership the Prussians carried out a general retreat. Some prickly individuals such as von Stülpnagel at Sombreffe served to break the waves of assaillants. Soon afterwards calm returned, the rain stopped and the storm moved on. Napoleon left the battlefield in the region of half past nine.

The French camped on the spot, surrounded by the dead and wounded. Napoleon had lost some 9,600 men and Blücher left some 16,000 dead and wounded on the field. Approximately 10,000 others had simply disappeared. Only 600 Prussians surrendered and barely 30 artillery pieces fell into French hands.

Napoleon had deployed his forces in depth and engaged his various echelons progressively. Even though the Ligne formed a first-class barrier Blücher left far too many men behind it downstream of Boignée. The old field marshal engaged his units sparingly and prematurely and soon found himself without any reserves. As for Napoleon, he maintained a reserve until the end. Thus, the 6$^{th}$ corps took no part in the battle. In addition, Napoleon used his artillery *en masse* while Blücher had his guns scattered all over the place.

Ligny was only a minor victory since d'Erlon's corps was not involved due to defective communications. However, the fact that the Prussians did not lose their heads was not without significance.

*The Scots Greys*
*engaging the*
*Cuirassiers*
*(Lithograph after*
*R. Simkin : MRA*
*collection).*

# CHAPTER VII

# 17th June : Marches and Countermarches

## The Prussian Retreat

**A**fter Ligny Gneisenau decided to retire in the direction of Wavre. The following day Blücher confirmed this decision from Mellery, where he had been taken. In deciding to march towards Wavre the Prussians made a junction with Wellington's forces possible. A withdrawal via Namur towards their base in Liège seemed logical but, had they done so, they would have exposed their flank to a French attack.

Early in the morning the 2$^{nd}$ corps at Gentinnes was ordered by Gneisenau to move towards Wavre via Mont-Saint-Guibert. The 1$^{st}$ corps followed from Tilly, a move representing a total of 39,000 men. The 3$^{rd}$ corps, which left Sombreffe for Wavre via Gembloux, Walhain and Corbais, was soon joined by the 4$^{th}$. These two corps totalled 52,000 men. Taken separately, each of the two armies formed by Gneisenau was numerically stronger than Grouchy's shadowing force. One brigade covered the retreat in the vicinity of Mont-Saint-Guibert. The 4$^{th}$ corps reached Dion-Valmont late in the evening. The Prussian troops were now concentrated in the vicinity of Wavre, where they had also set up their central depot. The replenishment of supplies could now begin.

## French initiatives

The Emperor read Ney's report on the battle of Quatre-Bras at nine in the morning at the Château de la Paix in Fleurus, where he had spent the night. At approximately the same time he received the first information from Grouchy on the Prussians' retreat. On the basis of this information he estimated that Blücher was withdrawing to Gembloux, Namur and Liège.

At about half past ten Napoleon decided to place Grouchy at the head of an army consisting of the 3rd and 4th corps and Exelman's and Pujol's cavalry — a total of 33,000 men and 96 guns. He gave the order to pursue Blücher and to prevent him from joining up with Wellington. Napoleon had badly overestimated the Prussians' losses, believing that they only had about 30,000 men who had got away and were ready to fight.

Accompanied by the Guard, the 6th corps and Milhaud's, Domon's and Subervie's cavalry, Napoleon was going to march towards Quatre-Bras to join Ney, and together they would undertake a flanking movement against Wellington. Considering that just over 70,000 men and 240 guns should be enough to carry out this new manoeuvre, he left the rest of Girard's division at Ligny.

Grouchy's troops set off in pursuit at two in the afternoon. At about three it began to rain hard. The sunken lanes became less and less practicable. The 3rd and 4th corps reached Gembloux in the evening. Whilst Exelmans' cavalry was at Sauvenière, Teste's division had scarcely reached Mazy. In the meanwhile it became obvious to Grouchy that Blücher was withdrawing in the direction of Wavre. He informed Napoleon of this and confirmed that he would prevent the junction of Wellington's and Blücher's forces.

Wellington learnt of the result of the battle of Ligny at seven in the morning. He also knew that Blücher would withdraw towards Wavre. He therefore decided to evacuate Quatre-Bras and concentrate his troops a dozen kilometres further north on the Mont Saint Jean plateau, where he had decided to fight. Blücher had promised him the support of an army corps at least. If this aid did not materialise he would evacuate Brussels and retire behind the Scheldt. At ten o'clock the allies set off along the Brussels and Nivelles roads, with the bulk of the infantry marching across the fields parallel to the road as was the custom.

Ney did not realise what was going on and did nothing for the whole of the morning. Napoleon set off with his troops around midday, but the British cavalry and horse artillery were forming a screen to the north and south of the allies. The succession of hills provided them with so many excellent positions. At about two o'clock Napoleon had to deploy his troops, but shortly afterwards a violent storm broke and the British cavalry retired along three axes via Loupoigne, Baisy-Thy, and the main road.

Napoleon took over the command of Ney's troops and the French set off northwards again with the cavalry in the van. They were followed by d'Erlon's 1st corps, and the 2nd brought up the rear.

The ally contrived to gain a maximum of time in the Genappe bottleneck, with the French advance being interrupted for a time by cannon-fire and rockets as well as by the narrow streets and the 2.5 metre-wide bridge across the Dyle.

The French were once again forced to deploy their troops to the north of Genappe. At about half past six Napoleon reached the Belle Alliance. Milhaud's cuirassiers were received near La Haie-Sainte by the brisk fire of 60 guns and Napoleon realised that it was there that Wellington wanted to fight.

# CHAPTER VIII

# Waterloo:
# The day of reckoning

## The night of 17th June

**A**fter suffering defeat, retreating overnight and spending a day on the march the Prussians finally succeeded in concentrating their forces in the vicinity of Wavre — the 1$^{st}$ corps at Bierges, the 2$^{nd}$ at Sainte-Anne, the 3$^{rd}$ at La Bawette and the 4$^{th}$ at Dion-le-Mont. Blücher's headquarters were in Wavre itself. A rearguard remained at Mont-Saint-Guibert.

Further to the west Hill's 1$^{st}$ corps was resting near Braine-l'Alleud while the 2$^{nd}$, under Prince William of Orange, was in the vicinity of Mont-Saint-Guibert. The Prince himself was at the Abeiche farm. A large body of 15,000 men and 320 guns under Prince Frederick of Orange was scattered over a considerable area including Halle, Braine-le-Château, Oisquercq and Bierges. Their task was to protect the line of communication to the coast. Wellington set up his headquarters opposite the church in Waterloo, in a charming inn — the *Jean de Nivelles* — now tranformed into a museum. A medical unit moved into the old Hospitallers' farm. These hospitallers probably gave their name to the hamlet of Mont-Saint-Jean.

*Epinal's prints lost no time in spreading the legend that "The Guard dies. It does not surrender" (MRA collection).*

93

The British paid for the food that they received from the local inhabitants as a supplement to their own supplies. Some of the officers lodged with the "natives".

The main bodies of Wellington's and Blücher's armies were thus concentrated around Mont-Saint-Jean and Wavre respectively. Their headquarters were about fifteen miles apart as the crow flies.

On the French side no orders had been issued to bivouac. Napoleon did not issue any and Soult probably did not dare. Most of the French army's bivouacs were scattered between the Belle Alliance and Quatre-Bras. In the Belle Alliance itself — a building dating from the middle of the XVIII century which owed its name to the marriage of the owner and his servant — Baron Percy established a small field hospital. The $3^{rd}$ and $4^{th}$ corps and Exelmans' and Pajol's cavalry spent the night as well as they could in the Baudeset, Grand-Leez, Mazy and Ernage area. Grouchy, their commander, lodged in Gembloux, about twenty kilometres as the crow flies from Le Caillou farm, where Napoleon had quartered himself. The rest of the unfortunate Girard's division had been retained in Fleurus.

Total devastation reigned wherever the French pitched their camp and the Prussians passed. The inhabitants either fled to the north or sought refuge in the woods with their belongings. All that could be found were miserable, almost empty houses with cob walls and thatched roofs. The night in question was cold and dark, and it was raining. The French troops had to pillage to find food. The wet branches collected in the woods or along the roadside burnt badly and the men had to fall back on the few pieces of furniture that they found here and there. More than one cavalryman slept leaning against his horse's warm belly. A lot of discussion went on in the bivouacs. The word treachery was on everybody's lips. Prince Jérôme, General Reille and his divisional commanders spent the night at the *Roi d'Espagne*, where Wellington had breakfasted. Napoleon lodged with his staff at the XVI century Le Caillou farm in the hamlet of *Les Flamandes*. The Brunswickers had caused some terrible damage and only a frightened female servant remained. Henri-Joseph Boucqueau, the aged proprietor, had fled. In 1819 he sold the ruins. Today, Le Caillou belongs to the tourist department of the Province of Brabant-Wallon. When Napoleon arrived, his servants put everything into order and set up the imperial bed for the night. The Emperor dined with Ney and a number of his generals.

Towards nine o'clock Napoleon received a report from Milhaud announcing the advance of a Prussian column towards Wavre via Géry and Gentinnes. But he could not believe that Blücher would attempt to join Wellington.after suffering defeat and after Grouchy's pursuit. He retired to bed without inspecting the front line, and the generals bedded down on the straw in the neighbouring rooms. The guard was entrusted to the 1st batallion of the 1st *Chasseurs à Pied* of the Guard under the command of lieutenant-colonel Duuring, a native of the Netherlands. The password was "Biron-Brest-Bonté".

After the meal Ney returned to his own headquarters at Chantelet, an estate some 1,500 metres to the east of Le Caillou and now the property of the Solvay family.

## The Site

In September 1814 Wellington had already undertaken a detailed reconnaissance of the terrain and believed that it was the right place to halt an invading French army. Moreover, the strategic interest of the place had also been recognised by the Austrian General Ferraris who, in 1777, had drawn up the first reliable map of the southern Netherlands for his emperor. After their defeat at Fleurus in 1794 the Austrians had tried to block the French advance at Mont-Saint-Jean.

A sort of rampart was formed by a ridge some 1.30 metres high that ran in an arc from Fichtermont to Smohain and then

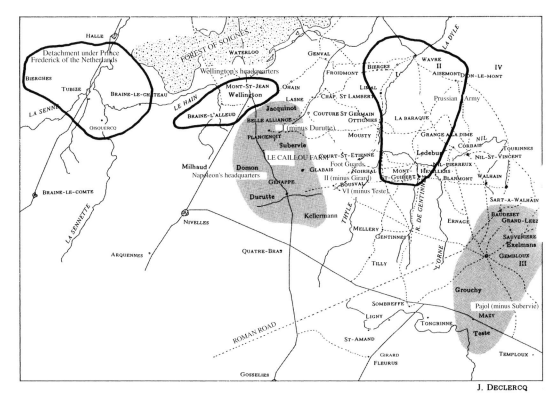

J. DECLERCQ

*Waterloo, the armies' positions on the 17th & 18th June.*

followed the Ohain lane to Braine-l'Alleud. Running from east to west, this ridge was broken in the centre by the paved Brussels-Charleroi road, 5-6 metres wide and bordered with elms. The southward slope was steep to begin with and then gradual. It became more pronounced at the bottom of the valley and then tailed off over some 600 metres. Behind the ridge the terrain fell away towards the north and lost itself in the Forest of Soignes. In 1815 Waterloo lay in the shadow of the forest, so as to speak. Access was by four paved roads, various dirt tracks and the gaps between the high beech trees. The Nivelles road started from the hamlet of Mont-Saint-Jean.

The road that ran along the ridge from Ohain to Braine-l'Alleud consisted partly of a sunken lane — sometimes 3-4 metres deep — lined with thick bushes. Today, this sunken lane has virtually disappeared. The banks have been levelled and the earth used to erect the mound surmounted by the Lion. The high ground upon which the King's German Legion and

Gordon memorials stand gives an idea of the lie of the land at the time. Forward of the bulwark formed by the sunken lane and the ridge there were four strongpoints — the huge rectangular brick and sandstone Brabantine farms of La Haie, La Papelotte, La Haie-Sainte and Goumont. To the east of the main road, between La Haie-Sainte and the crossroads, there was a sandpit. Two ditches completed the picture. There is a stream on either side of the battlefield — the Smohain in the east that flows into the Lasne, and another in the west that flows into the Hain. The watershed between the two is 130 metres above sea level and forms the gateway onto the site. Beyond a 1,300-metre valley barely 20 metres deep at its eastern end there is the paved Brussels-Charleroi road and, to the south, a small inn called the Belle Alliance. South of the Belle Alliance the watershed between the Senne and Dyle basins swings away in a north-westerly direction and leaves the countryside almost flat.

The battlefield itself lies in the districts of Braine l'Alleud, Lasne and Waterloo. It is not particularly large, measuring barely 2.5 kilometres from north to south and five from east to west.

Approximately two thirds of the fields were cultivated and, apart from a little clover, the crops were mainly rye, oats and

*The village of Plancenoit, where the French and Prussians fought on the 18th June until nightfall (Lithograph by Sturm according to Pingret, MRA collection).*

barley. These could grow to more than 1.50 metres in height, but were less compact than today. The remaining fields were left fallow and were overrun with weeds. The whole area was scattered with hawthorn hedges and the ground was sticky and slippery when it was wet.

On the 18th June the sun rose at 3.48 am. There was a slight breeze and the day looked as though it would be fine.

Behind the southern ridge and to the east of the main road in the direction of the Lasne there is the small village of Plancenoit. There was a certain number of obstacles between Wavre and the Waterloo battlefield, and particularly the Bois de Paris wood and the Lasne. There were no paved roads in the area. The town of Wavre was situated mainly on the north-western bank of the Dyle, and two stone bridges linked it to its south-eastern district. There was a paved road from Brussels to Wavre, which continued as a dirt road in the direction of Namur.

## Preparations

At 2 am Wellington got up and wrote some letters. He asked Frances Webster, his mistress, to make preparations to leave Brussels for Antwerp if the need arose; he ordered the commander of the Antwerp garrison to declare a state of siege and to prepare for the arrival of the French royal family and a number of British families and other foreigners; he requested Louis XVIII to move to Antwerp if Brussels fell into Napoleon's hands; finally, he recommended the British ambassador in Brussels to prepare a British withdrawal, but without haste or panic since things could still turn out well.

At 3 o'clock he received a letter that Blücher had written an hour earlier. The old field marshal promised to attack Napoleon's right flank with one, and perhaps even three, army corps. Wellington therefore decided to fight.

*The main building at Hougoumont with the built-on chapel. This building was set alight during the battle and collapsed, burying the many wounded inside (MRA collection).*

Blücher sent Bülow's still intact 4th corps along the old Wavre-Nivelles road towards Chapelle-Saint-Lambert. Following this, the 1st corps was to move via Froidmont and Ohain. The 3rd, which had scarcely been engaged at Ligny, was to pin down Grouchy on the Dyle at Wavre. At Gneisenau's insistance — he was extremely distrustful of Perfidious Albion — the troops despatched to aid the British were ordered not to intervene before the latter were fully engaged. Blücher suggested that he and the allies take the initiative the following day if the French did not attack on the 18th.

At five o'clock that morning Wellington mounted *Copenhagen*, his chestnut thoroughbred. He was neatly dressed as usual, without braid or plumes. His bicorne, which he wore fore and aft, was decorated with the British, Dutch, Portuguese and Spanish cockades. He issued his orders beneath the large elm at the south-west corner of the crossroads formed by the Brussels road and the Ohain-Braine-l'Alleud lane. In 1818 J. Children, a British businessman, bought the tree and cut it up to make two chairs and also numerous little souvenirs which brought him in a tidy sum. One of the chairs he presented to Queen Victoria and the other to the Duke of Wellington. The latter is still in the Duke's residence at *Aspley House*.

William of Orange was also beneath the elm to receive his orders from the commander in chief. He was wearing the uniform of the British 10<sup>th</sup> Hussars, whose colonel he was. Of particular note was his dark blue dolman adorned with a white feather and an orange cockade.

Wellington disposed his troops so that his veterans supported the less solid units. The British formed the core of this body of some 67,000 men, 7,000 of whom were kept at Braine-l'Alleud, a few kilometres to the west. Wellington set up his foward line with a centre and two wings, keeping the reserves under his direct command. The right wing extended towards the west from the point where the two roads to Braine-l'Alleud forked (the site of the present Panorama), and was placed under Hill. The track from Braine-l'Alleud to Rossomme was controlled by elements of the 15<sup>th</sup> Hussars. The right centre, which defended Mont-Saint-Jean, was commanded by the Prince of Orange and the left centre, to the east of the main road, was under Sir Thomas Picton. Further to the east, the left wing included part of the light cavalry, the rest being kept in reserve with the heavy cavalry. All these units were deployed behind the ridge. Fifty-eight guns were posted along the crest and approximately one hundred others were in reserve. Two brigades - Bijland's, which had already suffered badly, and Saxe-Weimar's — were stationed on the left centre and the extreme left respectively. They were positioned on the forward slope of the ridge that was visible to the French, and to the front of the La Papelotte and La Haie farms. The farms were occupied and loopholed. Some 1,200 men — Guards and units from Nassau and Hanover — were concentrated in the grounds of the manor-cum-farm of Hougoumont (or Goumont). In the centre, a thousand men of the King's German Legion fortified themselves in La Haie-Sainte, and a British batallion occupied the sandpit. The farms of La Papelotte, La Haie and the manor of Fichtermont were defended by the Prince of Saxe-Weimar's men. Some trees were cut down in the centre to block the main road.

Wellington's right wing was obviously more important than his left flank. This was because he was counting on Prussian help from that direction and, anyhow, he did not want to be cut off from the troops around Halle under Prince Frederick of the Netherlands.

Wellington's men prepared themselves for the great encounter. They discharged their muskets to dry the barrels and the pans, they lit fires, they ate, they drank tea and later they shared out the rum and the gin.

Napoleon slept badly during the night of the 17$^{th}$ June. Reports were arriving one after the other. At three o'clock he got up and immediately asked General Gourgaud to check whether the British were still there. In the meanwhile he learnt from a despatch from Grouchy written at eleven that evening that one Prussian column was moving towards Wavre via Sart-à-Walhain and another towards Perwez via Sauvenière; a body of troops was also fleeing in the direction of Namur.

At ten o'clock Napoleon ordered a message to be sent to Grouchy. It drew his attention to the Prussian column marching towards Wavre via Gentinnes that had been spotted by Milhaud's cavalry. It informed him that he would fight the British at Waterloo and added, "His Majesty thus desires you to direct your movements towards Wavre so as to draw closer to us, coordinate operations and maintain communications. You are to drive before you any corps of the Prussian army which has taken this direction and which may have halted at Wavre, where you must arrive as soon as possible (...). Inform me immediately of your dispositions, your marches and any information that you have on the enemy; do not fail to remain in communication with us. The Emperor desires to have frequent intelligence from you". Napoleon did not, therefore, expect Grouchy on the battlefield, but he did want to be kept informed of his movements and did not think that the Prussians would intervene. At eight o'clock he ate heartily in the company of Henri Bertrand, the marshal of his household, Soult, Ney,

Jérôme and Reille. Soult insisted on calling in some of Grouchy's troops as reinforcements. Napoleon displayed some impatience, calling Wellington a bad general and saying that he believed that he had a 90 % chance of success, and that the affair would soon be over.

He predicted that he would spend that night in Brussels provided that his orders were carried out meticulously. The conversation between allied officers overheard not long before at the *Roi d'Espagne* in Genappe and reported by his brother Jérôme did not particularly disturb him. How could a waiter know that the Prussians were hastening from Wavre and would join the British at the edge of the Forest of Soignes ? It was no doubt a trick. He swept any doubts under the carpet and ordered that the army be ready to fight at nine o'clock. He soon had to agree to the unrealistic nature of this order, however.

After the meal Napoleon courteously received the owner of Le Caillou who had returned, and who begged him to spare his property. He then requested that a "well-done" shoulder of mutton be prepared for him for six that evening, mounted his mare *La Marie* and, followed by his staff, visited the outposts. The troops applauded him wherever he went. He ordered

*Hougoumont rapidly became a place of pilgrimage for British visitors (Lithograph by Jobard after Pingret, MRA collection).*

d'Erlon to be ready towards midday. At eleven o'clock he sent out his orders from his observation post, a hillock 141 metres above sea level and situated to the east of the main road, near the Rossomme farm. Opposite was a smallholding owned by Jean-Baptiste Decoster, a peasant originally from Korbeek-Lo, whom Napoleon forced to furnish details of the terrain and the enemy.

Today the question of why Napoleon waited so long before attacking is a source of much interest. Was it to assemble all his troops ? Or did he want to let the ground dry out so that his guns could be moved more easily and the ricochets would have more effect ?

After receiving their orders the 70,000 men — 50,000 infantry and more than 5,000 gunners serving 240 guns — took up their positions They were deployed in a traditional geometric pattern, and in perfect order, over a 4,000-metre front with a depth of 1,200 metres. In the first echelon to the east of the main road Napoleon placed Drouet d'Erlon's 1$^{st}$ corps flanked by his cavalry on his right. To the west he placed Reille's 2$^{nd}$ corps, with Piré's cavalry on its left. In the second echelon Milhaud's cuirassiers and the cavalry were deployed to the east of the main road, on its immediate right, while Lobau's 6$^{th}$ corps was placed on its immediate left. The young Kellermann's cuirassiers, dragoons and carabiniers were drawn up further to the west. The third echelon consisted of the Foot Guards, whose twenty-four batallions were paraded in columns on either side of the main road. Finally, Lefèbvre-Desnouette's lancers and *chasseurs* were positioned further back, and on the right, with Claude Guyot's dragoons, horse grenadiers and gendarmes on the left. The distance between the different echelons was about 200 metres.

Napoleon also got together a huge artillery battery that he placed under the command of General Desvaux de Saint-Maurice, the commander of the Guards artillery. To begin with he had assembled 24 12-pounder guns, but he later increased their number considerably. Besides the 1$^{st}$ corps' 46 guns, he brought up the 2$^{nd}$ and 6$^{th}$ corps artillery and two Guards batteries, i.e. 30 12-pounders, 28 mainly 6-pounders, some 8-pounders and 20 mortars — 78 guns in all. This "grand battery" — his *ultima ratio* — was positioned on the Belle Alliance ridge, to the east of the main road and forward of the 1$^{st}$ corps.

The spectacle as the troops moved into place was magnificent. Formations snaked across the terrain like huge serpents while the numerous bands played the *Marseillaise* and *Veillons au salut de l'Empire*. Napoleon set the beginning of the engagement at about 1 pm due to the large number of units arriving late on the field.

With the troops in position the French and the Anglo-Dutch seemed to have created two opposing concave arcs. The adversaries were separated by some 1,300 metres on the central axis formed by the main road, and by about 200 metres at either end, i.e. the La Haie farm in the east and Goumont in the west.

Napoleon's plan was fairly simple. After the great battery had pounded the British centre d'Erlon's still intact 1$^{st}$ corps would try and break through, with the main thrust coming from Quiot's division, that was posted on the far left. The 2$^{nd}$ corps would cover its left flank. The objective was the Mont-Saint-Jean crossroads. Once it was reached, the pioneers would start fortification work. Napoleon was applying the methods used for overrunning strongpoints, but Mont-Saint-Jean was a bastion.

The task of leading the attack fell to Marshal Ney. Why did Napoleon choose the Prince of the Moskova, whom he called the "Bravest of the Brave ?" Was it because of his reputation for courage amongst the men ? Because he intended that he should pay with his life ? Or so that he could make amends for his "treachery" at the time of Napoleon's abdication, his support for Louis XVIII, and his relatively mediocre performance at Quatre-Bras ?

Certain authors suggest a much more subtle plan — the combination of a breakthrough and an outflanking movement around La Papelotte that Napoleon dreamt of on St. Helena. But there is nothing in the way of documents, facts or evidence to give credence to this theory.

# The Battle

Napoleon stayed at his observation post, sitting on a rattan chair with Chanlaire & Capitaine's map spread out on a farmhouse table in front of him. He regularly viewed the battlefield through a telescope. Soult stood on his left, and his staff remained at a respectful distance. The Emperor did not leave before five in the afternoon. He then went for a short time to another hillock, also 141 metres above sea level, situated to the east of the Belle Alliance. At seven he again absented himself from his observation post for a while before he was forced to flee.

## The Struggle against the Allies between 11 am and 6.30 pm

As was the custom, the Guards artillery fired three shots to announce the start of the battle — but for the last time. It was 11.35. The grand battery immediately opened up on the British positions.

Around about ten to one Soult spotted something unusual in the direction of Chapelle-Saint-Lambert and informed Napoleon. At the same time the Emperor received a letter that Grouchy had sent at six that morning with the following message: "Sire, all my intelligence reports confirm that the enemy is retiring in the direction of Brussels either to concentrate his forces or to fight after joining up with Wellington".

*Following pages:*
*The meeting of the two*
*victors on the evening*
*of Waterloo*
*(MRA collection).*

105

R. KNÖTEL.

The news from Grouchy and Milhaud and the conversation reported by his brother were all swirling around in Napleon's head. Shortly afterwards an NCO of the 2$^{nd}$ Silesian Hussars was brought before him. He was to hand Wellington a letter from Bülow announcing the arrival of the 4$^{th}$ Prussian corps. The intercepted letter and the avowal obtained from the NCO admitted of no further doubt as to a Prussian intervention.

Napoleon immediately despatched General Bernard, his ADC, to the east, and the general soon confirmed the Prussians' approach. Their infantry could cover the 8 kms or so to the battlefield in three hours. The Emperor hoped to obtain a decision in that time.To raise his troops' morale he had the rumour spread that Grouchy was approaching. However, he also had a message sent to Grouchy, timed 1 pm but sent an hour later, which read "You must keep manoeuvering in our direction and seek to draw nearer to the army so as to be able to join us before any corps places itself between us. I do not indicate to you any special direction; it is for you to ascertain the point where we are, to act accordingly, to keep up our communications and to see that you are constantly in a position to fall upon and to annihilate any of the enemy's troops which might try to molest our right". He enclosed Bülow's letter. When would Groucy receive this message? Between six and seven at the very earliest! It was therefore impossible for the marshal to reach the battlefield before nightfall.

The Prussians entered the Bois de Paris wood after an engagement involving the death Colonel von Schwerin, the commanding officer of the 1$^{st}$ cavalry brigade of the 4$^{th}$ corps. But instead of pushing on they waited, on Gneisenau's express orders, for the battle to be well under way before they intervened. You never know with the British!

The Emperor reckoned that he still had a 60% chance of emerging victorious. He sent Domon's and Subervie's cavalry to the Bois de Paris and followed them up with Lobau's 6$^{th}$ corps. Lobau's task was to position himself so as to be able to contain 30,000 men with his 10,000.

*The Belle Alliance tavern where Wellington and Blücher apparently met after the battle (Lithograph by an unknown artist. MRA collection).*

Napoleon then decided to launch his main assault, but his attention was diverted to Goumont. This large farm, now transformed into a redoubt, appeared on Ferraris' map as "Hougoumont", but this is a phonetic transcription of "au Goumont". The earliest traces of the property date back to the

XIV century; today, it belongs to the d'Oultremonts and is worked by the Temmerman family. In 1815 the property consisted of a manor house at the northern end, with an avenue of trees linking it to the Nivelles road. To the east there was an orchard and a French-style garden surrounded by a wall and, to the south, a 5-hectare wood. The farm proper was built onto the manor house.

What took place at Goumont? The Emperor had doubtlessly ordered his brother to create a diversion to cause the British to reinforce to their right wing to the detriment of their centre. But what was intended as a diversion was soon to turn into a bloodbath.

Jérôme's artillery opened up at 11.35. The British artillery answered, leading to a riposte from part of Reille's artillery and some of Kellermann's guns. Piré's cavalry attacked from the Nivelles road. The French infantry succeeded in overrunning the wood but could not break down the south gate. Their front soon came under fire from the farm, and their flank from the garden. To all this was added the shrapnel fired on Wellington's orders. This concentration of fire caused numerous losses amongst the attackers, including General Bauduin, the commander of the leading brigade. In the meanwhile Wellington replaced the Nassau troops by most of the King's German Legion and the greater part of Byng's and Du Plat's brigades.

At midday Jérôme ordered a new attack. The south gate seemed to be impregnable. The French therefore crept along the walls on the west side of the building to get to the north gate, which had been left open so that reinforcements could get in. The defenders suceeded in closing it in extremis, but Lieutenant Legros, a giant nicknamed *L'Enfonceur*, smashed the hinges of one side of the double door with an axe and the attackers rushed in. Violent hand to hand fighting ensued in the buildings, in the corridors, in the garden and even in the chapel. MacDonnell succeeded in repulsing the attackers and barricading the gate. A single French drummer was taken prisoner. In the meanwhile Jérôme's 2$^{nd}$ brigade had occupied the orchard, but the garden's defenders hung on. The shrapnel was creating ravages in the French ranks. A counter-attack, launched by the Coldstream Guards, drove the French out of the orchard. Time was passing. It was now half past one, and Wellington made use of a pause and the shelter provided by a fold in the ground to replace the most sorely tried troops.

At about 2 o'clock Jérôme launched another attack at almost the same time as the 1$^{st}$ corps' major assault. The fate of his family was at stake. For *König Lustik* [6] it was a matter of life or death. In addition to the 6$^{th}$ division, elements of Foy's division were also engaged. The orchard once again fell into the hands of the French, but this time they did not succeed in getting round the buildings.

Now wounded, Jérôme realised that the bastion could not be carried without artillery. At about three in the afternoon Napoleon sent him a mortar battery. By firing shells on a curved trajectory the French managed to set the buildings alight. Only the main building, the south gate and the chapel were undamaged — at least partly. Numerous wounded died in the flames — 304 Coldstream Guardsmen and 239 men of the 3$^{rd}$ Scots Guards perished or were seriously injured. Today the chapel remains a moving witness to so much suffering.

Goumont held out despite everything. Some 4,000 soldiers immobilised some 8,000 French. The fighting in the woods ceased at nightfall and the general retreat of the French.

During this time the grand battery was still firing. The distance to the most advanced positions was between 800 and 1,300 metres. The 12- 8- and 6-pounder guns could carry as far as 1,800, 1,500 and 1,200 metres respectively provided that they were loaded with a maximum charge of powder and fired at an elevation of 45 degrees, but the drift was considerable and ricochets non-existent. But ricochets were precluded anyhow

*Following pages: "I have recovered from my fall (...) our victory is the most complete that has ever been won (...) Napoleon slipped away during the night without either his hat or his sword (...) I am today sending his hat and his sword to the King" (Field Marshal Blücher's letter to his wife, dated from Gosselies on 20$^{th}$ June 1815).*

---

6. Because of his frivolity *König Lustik* (the Merry Monarch) received this nickname when he was King of Westphalia. Napoleon criticised him for this frivolity.

by the reverse gradient and the spongy ground. Only Bijland's brigade and the British artillery posted along the crest of the ridge were badly hit. It was rare for a shot to go over the top.

At one o'clock Napoleon gave Ney the order to attack. The deployment of the four divisions of the 1st corps — some 17,000 men — was remarkable. The left-hand division, commanded by Quiot, formed into two columns — one per brigade. Each column consisted of four batallions, with each pair of batallions marching at a distance of six paces from the other and forming three ranks of between 120 and 150 metres from end to end. The second column was 200 metres from the first and slightly to the rear. Quiot's division had La Haie Sainte as its objective. The other three divisions each formed a column of eight or nine batallions that had the appearance of a succession of slender phalanxes. This is what was known as *columns of batallions by divisions*. However, there was also the much more supple formation consisting of *columns of divisions by batallions* — a checkerboard arrangement of batallion columns, each of which was made up of two companies marching abreast and extending nine ranks to the the rear. The gap made it possible to form squares. Was the mistakenly adopted formation due to a badly understood verbal order ?

Donzelot's division followed a short distance behind Quiot's, but 400 metres ahead of Marcognet's. The bands started to play the *Pas de charge* and the men sang and shouted as they made their way through the crops. The grand battery fell silent for a moment and only started firing again when the men had dipped down into the valley. The divisional artillery moved forward in the narrow gaps and Travers' 450-man cuirassier brigade advanced to the left of the main road.

The brunt was taken by the five companies of the King's German Legion holding La Haie-Sainte under Major Baring, and by the riflemen of the 95th Foot defending the sandpit. Bijland's brigade came under artillery fire. Picton had ordered his infantry to lie down in the rye 150 metres to the rear of the ridge.

The left-hand French brigade headed by Quiot himself got into the orchard to the south of La Haie-Sainte, encircled the rectangle formed by the farm buildings, and tried to force the gates. The oldest part of the building dates back to the XVI century and was hardly damaged in 1815. The farm belongs to the Cornet d'Elzius de Chenoy family and is currently worked by the Van Achters. Quiot's other brigade, led by General Bourgeois, stormed he sandpit. The riflemen had to evacuate it and retire behind the ridge. The reinforcements sent by Wellington were useless because the garden to the north of La Haie-Sainte soon fell into the hands of the French as well. Bijland's units retired under pressure from Donzelot and Marcognet reached the Ohain lane. In the meanwhile Durutte had evinced Saxe-Weimar's men from La Papelotte.

It was difficult to deploy so as to be able to fire at all effectively. Fire directed at Donzelot's flank by James Kempt's brigade at scarcely 30 metres was followed by a bayonet attack under Picton's direction. This had the effect of repulsing the French. But Picton was mortally wounded and died around two o'clock a few metres from the site of the present-day monument to the "Hanoverians" which, in fact, is dedicated to the King's German Legion. Having arrived without any of his kit, the general was wearing civilian clothes at the moment of the attack. As for Marcognet, his division came under fire from the 92$^{nd}$ Highlanders at a range of 20 metres. It was then subjected to an assault carried out by Pack's brigade to the sound of the bagpipes. Donzelot's and Marcognet's divisions became intermingled to the extent that they soon degenerated into a shapeless mass from which only a few men could fire.

Placing himself at the head of Somerset's heavy brigade, Uxbridge gave the order for the cavalry to charge. The Household Brigade consisted of the 1$^{st}$ and 2$^{nd}$ Life Guards, the 1$^{st}$ Dragoon Guards and the Royal Horse Guards, otherwise known as the "Blues". After the charge was sounded seven squadrons attacked the French cavalry to the west of the main road. Despite their longer sabres the cuirassiers could not compete with their enemies because the British horses were bigger, more solid and better trained that the French ones. Travers' horsemen beat a retreat, dragging along part of Quiot's division that was near La Haie Sainte. Two batteries of horse artillery went belly up. Most of the Household brigade then turned back under the cover of the two squadrons kept in reserve. But, carried away by their enthusiasm, some elements of the Life Guards and the Dragoon Guards ventured too far south and were cut to pieces by the French cuirassiers and Bachelu's infantry.

In the meanwhile, to the east of the main road William Ponsonby had rushed into the attack at the head of the nine squadrons of the Union Brigade, i.e.the rest of the heavy cavalry. The English Royal Dragoons forced Quiot's infantry to retreat. Assisted by Corporal Stiles, Captain Kenney Clark succeeded in seizing the eagle of the 105th Infantry. The Irish Inniskilling Dragoons repulsed Donzelot. The Scots Greys — officially the 2nd Royal North British Dragoons and today the Royal Scots Dragoon Guards — drove in Marcognet's division. Sergeant William Ewart was even able to take the emblem of the 45th Infantry.

*Waterloo. The positions of the armies at about 11.30 on the 18th June.*

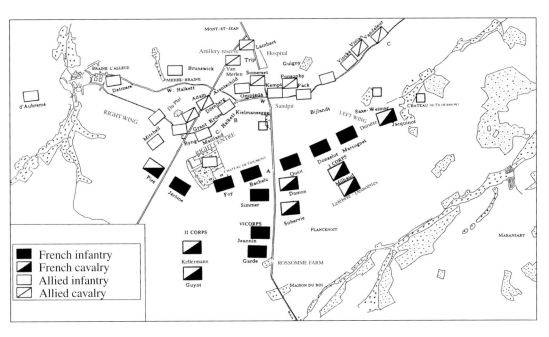

The British were quite carried away, with the Scots Greys galloping as far as the grand battery and spiking thirty guns. They then wanted to return to their own lines, but Farine's cuirassiers from Milhaud's army corps attacked them from the west and Jacquinot's lancers drove in their flank from the east. William Ponsonby was taken prisoner by Sergeant Urban of the 4th Lancers. As the British dragoons were about to rescue him the sergeant shot him dead with a pistol just in front of La Haie Sainte.

In the meantime the British had retaken La Papelotte thanks to the not inconsiderable help provided by Vandeleur's three regiments of light dragoons supported by Ghigny's Belgian hussars and the Dutch light dragoons. This cavalry was then able to provide cover for the retreat of the Union brigade. Colonel Frederick Ponsonby of the 12th Light Dragoons was seriously wounded during this fighting.

Durutte's division was much less hard hit by the cavalry charges and the fighting around La Papelotte. It is true that Durette had modified his troops' deployment at just the right moment, placing them in 150 files in line abreast.

It was now three o'clock, and the French attack had failed due to a lack of cavalry support. Time was passing. It was estimated that d'Erlon had lost some 5,000 men, including 3,000 prisoners taken by the British. But the British success had cost them dear. Their heavy cavalry had practicallly ceased to exist. About a thousand of the 2,500 or so men engaged were either dead or seriously wounded. Wellington had every reason to thank the survivors of the Household Cavalry as they passed near him in returning to their positions.

The two sides strove to collect their units together and to put them back in position. The rule concerning continuity of action had escaped the attention of the French. Time was on the side of the British. When would the Prussians arrive on the field ? In the meanwhile desertions were increasing alarmingly, and particularly in the Nassau contingent. On the French side the gendarmerie had their hands full arresting the fugitives. The grand battery was still firing without interruption, and the allies were answering as best they could. Lieutenant General Desvaux de Saint-Maurine was cut in two by one of their shells.

At about half past three Napoleon received the message that Grouchy had written at eleven o'clock at Sart-à-Walhain (now Walhain-Saint-Paul). It was clear from this message that the Emperor could expect no assistance from Grouchy since the latter did not anticipate reaching Wavre before the evening. At that particular moment the Prussians were about twelve hours ahead of Grouchy's troops. Since they could only march at a rate of 2.5 kms an hour the French had progressively dropped back until they were some thirty kilometres behind.

It was four o'clock when the rain finally stopped. Under Ney's command, Quiot and Donzelot once again tried to take La Haie-Sainte. The marshal was under the impression that he had seen some British retiring towards the north and thought that they were beginning to leave the field. In fact they were

*Towards the end of the battle the Prince of Orange was slightly wounded at the spot where the Lion would later be erected. He received first aid in the Mont-Saint-Jean farm, where a first aid post had been organised (MRA collection).*

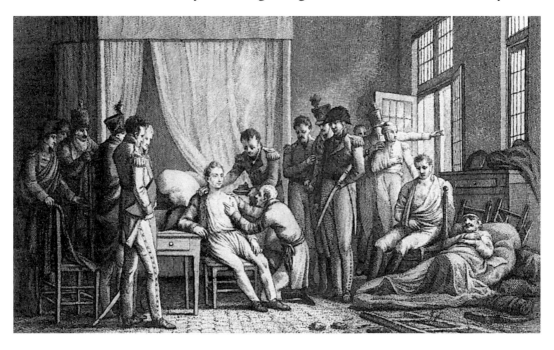

carrying off the wounded and trying to find cover behind the ridge. Ney had had the cavalry deployed since half past three and he now thought that the moment had arrived for them to attack. Milhaud's and Lefèbvre-Desnouettes' cavalry — a total of 5,000 sabres — had assembled near Goumont on the small ridge formed by the watershed between the Dyle and the Senne, These movements had not escaped Wellington's notice, however, and he had the sector between the two main roads reinforced and canister-firing guns brought up.

The marshy ground hardly lent itself to a cavalry charge. Because of the difficulty of deploying between La Haie-Sainte and Goumont, the drawing up of the squadrons left no room for surprise. Milhaud's divisions therefore formed themselves into squadron columns behind the Prince of the Moskova. While the grand battery had to stop firing, the British shrapnel began to rain down. The cavalry charged from approximately 100 metres. The infantry watched the performance without making any use of the cover provided by the cavalry. It is true that Ney had given no orders in this respect and that Napoleon was preoccupied with the Prussian danger. Once again there was no liaison between the infantry and the cavalry.

The British had double-loaded their guns with canister and solid shot. They opened fire when the enemy was about 45 metres away. While he first rank was almost entirely swept away by the canister, the solid shot ripped through the columns. The confusion was total and the gunners took advantage of it to seek shelter in the squares. The French seized some thirty guns, but they did not have the teams to haul them away or the nails to spike them. They could only break a rammer left behind in the gunners' haste to get alway.

The thirteen British squares (reference has been made to 18, but who knows now ?) formed a checkerkboard pattern 100 metres or so to the rear of the ridge. Wellington and his staff obtained a relative amount of protection by placing themselves in their midst. The British opened a murderous fire on the

*Following pages : The fighting on the 16th and 18th. June (Lithograph by F. Serz after P. G. Geister, MRA collection).*

119

NAPOLEON AN DER SPITZE SEINER GARDEN.

DIE

BLÜCHER'S PFERDESTURZ.

DER TOD DE

BLÜCHERS CAVALLERIE ANGRIFF.

BRAUNSCHWEIG.

NAPOLEON'S FLUCHT.

horses at a range of scarcely 20 metres, but the French cavalry just kept coming on and firing at a distance of 10-15 metres. Inside the squares the dead and wounded were piled up on top of each other. The acrid powder smoke was unbearable and the men were martyrs to thirst. The scene was Dantesque.

Uxbridge threw all his cavalry against the French flanks. Dörnberg, d'Arenschildt, van Merlen and Ghigny gave of their best. The French had no alternative but to retreat.

The French cavalry did not give up that quickly, however. A new charge was carried out by Lefèbvre-Desnouettes' division and the remainder of Milhaud's cavalry but the fire of the British artillery, which had retaken possession of their guns, dispersed it. The British squares were now hidden by dead Frenchmen and horses piled up around them.

In the meanwhile Napoleon had moved to a temporary observation post to the east of the Belle Alliance. It was five o'clock. He did not think that the cavalry charge without infantry and artillery coordination was a very good idea, but time was getting short because of the Prussians threat at Plancenoit. The Emperor therefore decided to have Kellermann's and Guyot's cavalry support Ney's attack. This took place at about half past five, with 10,000 horsemen launching a third series of charges in the stifling heat. Ney was everywhere, covered in perspiration and as red as a beetroot. "Old Redhead" earned his nickname — inspired by his red hair — more than ever. His clothes were in tatters. The British artillery was firing uninterruptedly. The square formed by the 69th Foot was shot to pieces. Three allied colours were lost. Wellington was becoming nervous and was playing with his telescope. Cumberland's hussars took to their heels and some 10,000 allied soldiers followed suit.

At all events, the fourth French charge was to no purpose. The phlegm of the British, the courage of the Germans and the tenacity of the Dutch were all remarkable. At six o'clock the

French cavalry retired, completely exhausted. And for half an hour calm appeared to return.

Ney finally decided to engage Bachelu's infantry and one of Foy's brigades — some 6,000 men in all. However, getting them into position took time. They had to cross 1,500 metres of devastated and muddy field covered with dead and dying men and horses — not an easy task. Surprise was non-existent. The British artillery fired shrapnel to begin with, then solid shot and, finally, the terrible canister. The French nevertheless reached the crest of the ridge and hand to hand fighting ensued. Colonel Karl Du Plat of the King's German Legion was killed. A brigade of Durutte's engaged to the east of La Haie-Sainte could not force a decision, either. A charge by the carabiniers succeeded in rescuing the infantry, but only at heavy cost. Once again the French lost numbers of the troops engaged — some 1,500 — in this new attack.

Since they blocked the French advance, Napoleon then decided to seize La Papelotte, La Haine and La Haie-Sainte whatever the cost. Durotte succeeded in retaking La Papelotte and La Haie with a single brigade. Supported by Quiot, Ney attacked La Haie-Sainte at the head of one of Donzelot's regiments and a company of engineers. The French succeeded in breaking in at the cost of enormous losses. Only forty-six uninjured Germans were able to escape. Most of the wounded were finished off on the spot. A battery of horse artillery then opened fire on the British centre 150 metres away. Colonel von Ompteda was killed in an attempted counter-attack. Most of the senior allied officers were either wounded or killed. William of Orange, nicknamed the *Little Frog,* was also wounded. He got off his horse and fainted. Captain T. de Constant Rebecque had him carried to the Hospitallers' farm at Mont-Saint-Jean. From there he was taken to the royal palace in Brussels.

During this time desertions from the allies' ranks were increasing. The men from the supply train fled in the direction of Brussels. The breakthrough seemed to have succeeded.

*The farm at Mont-Saint-Jean, where a British field hospital was set up on the morning of the 18th June (Lithograph by Willaume, after Lignian, MRA collection).*

Supported by some cavalry units, what remained of the 1st corps was poised to exploit the breach. The infantry, the cavalry and the artillery were cooperating at last. Ney asked the Emperor for reinforcements to carry out a decisive push towards the Mont-Saint-Jean crossroads. But Napoleon's right flank was giving way. It was half past six. What had happened?

## Prussian Killjoys

The Prussians had needed a lot of time to get from Wavre to Waterloo. It is true that the countryside was rather hilly and roads virtually non-existent. Also, Gneisenau wanted to engage the 4th corps first. This corps had remained intact, but it was located further away to the east and its units had to pass through the other corps' bivouacs. A fire in Wavre also held things up.

The Prussians finally appeared on the battlefield at about half past four. They were now convinced that Wellington would not let them down. Colonel von Pfuel had been following the battle from the western edge of the Bois de Paris wood, and both Blücher and Gneisenau subsequently came to observe events. They decided to attack Napoleon opposite the Guard — his final reserve — and the village of Plancenoit was selected as

*The Mont-Saint-Jean farm today.*

the objective. The time seemed to be right since the French cavalry was engaged in a merciless struggle at the other end of the field.

At about half past one French cavalry units under Domon and Subervie formed a screen on the western edge of the Bois de Paris. This choice of spot was not very wise because it was impossible to see towards the east. A position on the Lasne near Chapelle-Saint-Lambert would certainly have been far better. Lobau's 6th corps, which ran to only two small divisions of 7,000 men and 16 guns, had taken up position at Lasne, near the Bois de Ranson wood, to the north of the Plancenoit lane. Napoleon had engaged his second echelon to protect his flank.

The two leading brigades of Bülow's corps — those of Michael Losthin and Johann Hiller von Gärtringen — marched along the ridge from Genleau towards Plancenoit preceded by Prince William of Prussia's cavalry. In this way they could easily take their bearings from the roof of the Belle Alliance. A detachment on their right flank was despatched towards the Château de Fichtermont, where it set off in pursuit of a . . Nassau batallion. No doubt the similarity between the uniforms of the 1st Orange Nassau batallion and those of the French was the cause of this inter-German confrontation. However, contact was established with the allies shortly afterwards in the vicinity of La Haie.

After some skirmishing the French cavalry had retired behind the infantry. Fighting began towards five o'clock. The 13,500 Prussians pinned down the French in the Plancenoit lane at Genleau. This lane formed a sort of axis in this small-scale battle. Blücher moved two new brigades — those of Von Hacke and von Ryssel, totalling 14,000 men — from Aywières towards Plancenoit. Progress was very difficult in the Lasne valley, but this route meant that the French could be outflanked from the south. While Lobau had to retire hurriedly towards half past five to the immediate east of Plancenoit, one of his brigades moved into the village, which had some 500 inhabitants in 1815. The houses were fortified on their southern sides and Lobau could make contact with Durutte via his left flank.

The Prussians attacked Plancenoit from the east and the south. Their shot was soon falling in the surroundings of the Belle Alliance and Rossomme, on the Brussels-Charleroi road. Some of Napoleon's staff officers were wounded, and even killed. The French gave way before the numbers of Prussians, who soon occupied the part of Plancenoit in the valley near the church. The French hung onto the other part, where a monument to the Prussians now stands. A French battery positioned there caused serious damage to the enemy's serried ranks.

By way of reinforcements Napoleon sent in eight batallions of the Young Guard under Philippe Duhesme — some 4,000 men and 24 guns in all. After some hard fighting the 15th Prussian Infantry Regiment and the Silesian *Landwehr* were driven back, but a counter-attack by 7,000 men led by Hiller took the fighting back into the vicinity of the church. Subervie's lancers tipped the balance in favour of the French for a while, but the Prussians continued to pour in. Towards half past six Napoleon sent in part of the Old Guard in the shape of a batallion of *chasseurs* and one of grenadiers — more than a thousand men under the command of General Pelet. The cemetery was recaptured and the Prussians taken prisoner had their throats cut. Pelet was just able to save some of them from certain death. It was seven o'clock. The Franco-Prussian front ran from La Haie to some 600 metres to the east of Plancenoit. Lobau's troops were to the north, the Young Guard to the south, and the cavalry was in reserve. The two batallions of the Old Guard returned to Rossomme.

## Caught in a vice

Zieten's 1st corps arrived at Ohain via Genval at about six o'clock. The Prussian general felt seriously worried at the sight of allied soldiers fleeing from the battlefield. What should he do ? He decided to concentrate his troops and to wait. Shortly afterwards von Scharnhorst, Blücher's liaison officer, gave him the order to march on Plancenoit (Scharnhorst was a member of the family of the famous military reformer who had died of his

*The Prussians' march on 18th June. The fighting on the Dyle on the 18th and 19th June. The sitiuation at 3 pm on the 18th June.*

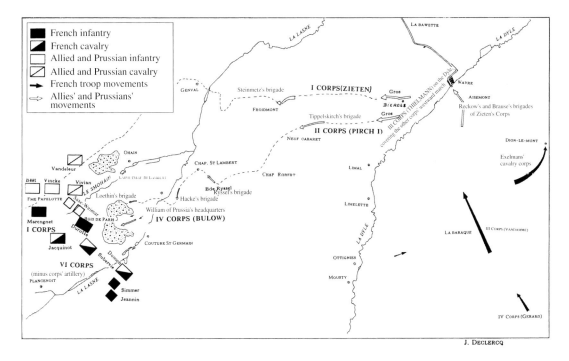

J. DECLERCQ

wounds in 1813). However von Müffling, Wellington's Prussian liaison officer, had now arrived on the scene. He reminded Zieten of the initial set of orders. Zieten hesitated, and then decided to act in accordance with the initial set. Time was running short.

Towards half past seven Ney pressed the Emperor once again for reinforcements. All that the Emperor had left was some nine Guards batallions, one battery and a few cavalry squadrons. Would be use them against the allies' wavering positions in the centre ?

At about the same time Chassé's division, hitherto in Braine-l'Alleud, arrived on the field from the west. Wellington immediately despatched it to reinforce his threatened centre. He did the same with the cavalry drawn in from the eastern flank where Zieten's Prussians had taken over. Wellington formed a semi-circular line from Goumont to the Braine-l'Alleud-Ohain and Brussels-Charleroi crossroads. He also spread the news that the Prussians had arrived and that an attack by the Guard had to be expected; a French deserter had warned him of this.

At about the same time Napoleon gave orders for a new attack on the allies' centre. He envisaged pushing Wellington back to the Forest of Soignes and then turning on the Prussians. Two hours seemed to be sufficient for this. The Guard was to spearhead the attack, Reille and d'Erlon were to protect the flanks and the cavalry would carry out small-scale charges. The grand battery and the horse artillery would intervene massively. Assisted by some gendarmes, General La Bédoyère was to spead the news that Grouchy had arrived. Morale had to be lifted. It took about half an hour to disseminate the orders.

In the meanwhile the Guard had gone into action. The Emperor followed the attack on foot from the main road. Six batallions of the Middle Guard under Ney advanced in columns

to the west of the road. Once again they followed the watershed. Four horse artillery guns accompanied the batallions in the spaces between them. One batallion halted near La Haie-Sainte while the other five continued their advance. In the second echelon there were three batallions of the Old Guard, some 1,500 men in all. Soldiers wandering about regained courage and grouped together behind the Guard. Everywhere the cry rang out "The Guard is attacking". Two batallions of the 1st Grenadiers of the Old Guard, a few sailors and pioneers and some squadrons of Napoleon's personal guard — about 1,200 men — were drawn up in reserve near the Decoster farm.

It was now eight o'clock. Anything was possible. The grand battery was firing continuously. The Guard moved imperturbably forward, followed by the remains of the French army. While Wellington incorporated all those who were still fit into his front line, the Belgo-Dutch force under General Chassé formed six squares behind the ridge. Wellington was

*The Pont du Christ bridge in Wavre, the prize in the furious fighting of the 18<sup>th</sup> June. (Lithograph by Sturm, after Pingret, MRA collection).*

everywhere. He is alleged to have said to the British "What would they say of us in England...?" This phrase no doubt translated the feelings of a large number of those present.

The Guard reached the crest of the ridge and the grand battery fell silent. The allied artillery's eleven batteries positioned in a semi-circle opened fire at a range of 200 metres with everything that they had. The Medium Guard reeled and, seeing this, Chassé's infantry attacked. On their western flank the British Guards rose up and a scarlet wall moved forward. The French endeavoured to hang on at Goumont and, particularly, at La Haie-Sainte, but what was left of the cavalry rushed in to the attack. The French were driven pitilessly back. A cry of disbelief and disappointment ran through the French ranks : "The Guard is retreating".

*Wellington's staff suffered some serious losses : Gordon, Lancey, Uxbridge etc. (F. Bromley after A. Cooper, MRA collection)*

## The Final Attack

Wellington raised his hat and waved it three times. For the allies, this was the signal to attack. Drums, bagpipes and fifes started to resound, adding something unreal to the drama of the moment. The allies then drove the French back. The squares of the Old Guard, which contained some legendary figures such as General Cambronne, were deployed near Decoster's farm, but they were unable to halt the waves of fugitives or, indeed, the enemy. The celebrated phrase "The Guard dies. It does not surrender" was never uttered by Cambronne. It was the invention of a journalist called Rougemont, who published it in the *Journal général de France* on 24<sup>th</sup> June. But, as is often the case, this type of remark is a true reflection of the spirit reigning in an elite formation at a crucial moment. Various counter-attacks launched by some squadrons of Napoleon's personal guard brought no relief. Cries of "treachery" and "Every man for himself" echoed all around. The lies concerning Grouchy's arrival were now rebounding against the Emperor. False hope degenerated into dispair. It was no longer possible to stop the debris of Drouet d'Erlon's and Reille's army corps as they fled. Only one brigade of Durutte's division was able to maintain good order and execute a fighting retreat under Ney.

During this time Pirch's 2<sup>nd</sup> Prussian corps was moving into Plancenoit. The balance of forces on Napoleon's right flank was very unequal. Bülow and Pirch had more than 30,000 infantry, 5,000 cavalry and more than 100 guns against scarcely 10,000 infantry, 2,000 cavalry and fifty guns. The intervention of Zieten's 1<sup>st</sup> corps near La Papelotte was the final straw.

It was now nine o'clock and darkness saved the retreating French. Napoleon sought refuge for a short time in one of the two squares formed near Rossomme by his last reserve. These two squares were full of generals and other officers. It was half past nine. In the darkness men fought to save their skins. One of the final shots from the last 12-pounder battery crushed Lord

Uxbridge's leg. That evening it was amputated and buried; the grave still exists in the garden of the Maison Paris, diagonally opposite the Wellington Museum in Waterloo. In 1880 it was transferred to Waterloo cemetery at the family's insistence.

Certain French generals wanted to die on the spot. What could they expect from a further restoration ? Napoleon left for Le Caillou. The few units that were still in one piece — particularly Duuring's batallion — also retired. Accompanied by a few officers Napoleon fled towards Genappe, where he found his carriage.


## A Meeting and a Breakaway

Wellington advanced as far as Le Caillou before deciding to order his exhausted troops to bivouac. The southernmost of their bivouacs were in the vicinity of Rossomme and La Maison du Roi. Returning to Waterloo, Wellington met Blücher near the Belle Alliance farm — or near La Maison du Roi, nobody knows exactly. Some sources say that Müffling acted as intermediary, and de Constant-Rebecq states that the meeting was between ten and eleven in the evening. Blücher wanted to name the battle La Belle Alliance since it seemed an appropriate name. Wellington preferred Waterloo, very probably because of its more English sound and since he had set up his headquarters there.

At this meeting it was also agreed that Gneisenau would continue the pursuit with 4,000 men, including Röder's cavalry. Towards midnight Pirch's 2nd corps would set off in the direction of Mansart to cut off Grouchy's retreat. Bülow would push on to Genappe, and Zieten would bivouac to the east of La Maison du Roi.

In Genappe the Emperor's carriage was marooned in a desperate mass of humanity trying to get away. The Prussians succeeded in capturing the carriage, but Napoleon managed to escape in time. By way of booty Major von Keller acquired a hat, a sword with a de luxe scabbard and a greatcoat. In the lining of the coat there were the diamonds that Pauline, the Emperor's sister, had sewn in. Subsequently the

Hohenzollerns would proudly adorn themselves with these diamonds.

The French took advantage of the night to flee under the protection of the Guards cavalry. The number of Prussian pursuers dwindled away. Gneisenau stopped south of Frasnes. Some 8,000 French had been taken prisoner. In the end only a single Prussian mounted drummer carried on the pursuit! Napoleon reached Charleroi at dawn. The rest of the army — some 30,000 men — regrouped and set off towards the south.

## A heavy toll

*Burying the dead near La Haie-Sainte. "Next to a battle lost, the greatest misery is a battle gained" (MRA collection).*

Next to a battle lost, the greatest misery is a battle gained. This remark — attributed to Wellington — is only too true. The battlefield was awful to contemplate - the smoking ruins of the buildings, the devastated fields and crops and the approximately ten thousand dead horses. In addition, there were about 7,000 French dead and, 4,800 allied (1,417 British,

1,226 Prussian, a thousand Belgian and Dutch, and 1,200 Germans and Dutch in the British service), and about three times as many wounded - some 40,000 in all. Thus, an overall total of some 50,000 were incapacitated in one way or another. Some well-known generals such as the British Picton and Ponsonby, the Belgian van Merlen and Collaert and the French Bauduin, Jean-Jacques Desvau de Saint-Maurice, Donop, Jamin and Michel were killed, and the French generals Cambronne, F. Lallemand and Lobau were taken prisoner.

The wounded passed through Mont-Saint-Jean farm, through various houses in the Mont-Saint-Jean hamlet, or through Joli-Bois. There were endless amputations — the only solution provided that no real infection had set in. The local inhabitants had to provide the allies with transport and, after the battle, were even requisitioned themselves. The French wounded were brought in last of all, with certain of them having lain out on the field for up to four days after the fighting — nine times out of ten stripped of everything, even their clothes. Even so, most of the wounded survived. Of those who ended up in a Brussels hospital only 9 % died.

*La Haie-Sainte.*

*Following pages:*
*Map of the Austrian*
*Netherlands drawn by*
*Count Ferraris.*
*Braine-l'Alleud*
*78 (F8)(4)*
*(Bibliothèque Royale*
*de Belgique).*

Many of the wounded were taken to the Brussels Military Hospital, an erstwhile Jesuit monastery. Other buildings — particularly the hospitals of Saint-Pierre and Saint-Jean, the Abbaye de la Cambre, the theatres and the churches of Sainte-Madeleine, Saint-Augustin and Les Béguines — were also crowded with wounded.

The dead were buried in large common graves and covered with quicklime and earth. Hundreds of corpses were burnt at Goumont.

# CHAPTER IX

# Wavre, June 18th

Grouchy wrote to Napoleon at six that morning informing him that the Prussians were very probably moving towards Wavre and that he would pursue them via Walhain and Corbais.

He left Gembloux with his troops during the morning. Exelmans' cavalry, which had left Sauvenière at six, was in the van and was followed by Vandamme's 3$^{rd}$ corps. Gérard's 4$^{th}$ corps moved off after eight. Pajol's cavalry and Teste's division had left Mazy towards 4 o'clock and were marching towards Wavre via Grand-Leeze and Tourinnes.

Grouchy arrived at Walhain at about nine. Some time later a certain Godseels, an ex-NCO of the *27$^{th}$ Chasseurs à Cheval* living in Perwez, warned him that the Prussians were in the vicinity of Wavre and that they intended to join Wellington to resume the struggle. Towards ten o'clock Grouchy established himself in Walhain-Saint-Paul at the Château de Longpré, the home of the notary Hollert. He wrote a letter to Napoleon that he sent off by courier at about half past eleven. In this letter Grouchy passed on the information provided by Godseels and confirmed by the notary. He said that he was going to march towards Wavre and requested further instructions.

*The Prussian monument surmounted by the Iron Cross. (Lithograph by Jobard, after Madou MRA collection).*

The marshal then accepted his host's offer of a light meal. He was enjoying some strawberries in the summerhouse when General Gérard suddenly burst in to tell him that the Emperor's guns could be heard in the west and that they should march in that direction. Gérard's tone was not very respectful and Grouchy was offended. He pointed out firstly that the sound of gunfire was normal since the Emperor was attacking the British, and secondly that his orders stated that he was to pursue the Prussians with the whole of his army. There was therefore no question of detaching the 4th corps in the direction of Waterloo. The Emperor's orders were clear. Furthermore, the terrain did not lend itself to any east-west movement. Not only were the dirt roads in a deplorable state, but the Dyle valley itself was a dangerous obstacle.

Blücher had re-assumed the command of the Prussian forces during the night of the 17th June. Shortly before midnight he explained the manoeuvre that he had in mind for the following day, and Gneisenau prepared the appropriate orders.

Bülow's 4th corps was to leave the heights of Dion-Valmont at dawn and march in the direction of Wavre, Neuf-

Cabaret, Chapelle-Robert and Chapelle-Saint-Lambert. Gneisenau laid down that the 4th corps must not be engaged until it was certain that Wellington was well and truly committed to battle. If this proved to be the case, the 4th corps would attack the French right flank. Pirch's 2nd corps would follow Bülow and support him. As for Zieten's 1st corps, it would reinforce Wellington's left flank after passing through Rixensart wood, Froidmont, Bourgeois and Genval, and to the left of Ohain.

Thielmann and his 3rd corps were to ensure freedom of action and prevent Grouchy's forces from crossing the Dyle at Wavre, Ottignies or Mousty.

At the same time, in a letter that Wellington would receive the next morning, Blücher promised to provide him with the aid that he required — two corps at least, even his whole army. If Napoleon did not attack on the 18th, the allies would be able to take the initiatve together on the 19th.

Bülow moved off at about four in the morning. Pirch struck camp towards midday, and Zieten two hours later. The sound of distant gunfire no doubt played a part in Pirch's setting off when he did.

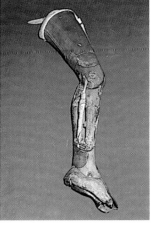

*Long after the battle British graves could still be seen in Waterloo cemetery. (Lithograph by G. Hunt fter M.E., MRA collection)*

*Lord Uxbridge, the Marquis of Anglesey's wooden leg. Gift to the Wellington Museum by the 7th Marquis of Anglesey.*

Bülow's 4$^{th}$ corps, which had not been engaged hitherto, was the first to take the offensive, but to do so it had to go through the 2$^{nd}$ corps' bivouacs. Bülow's advance guard reached Wavre at about 7 am. Four hours later some Prussian cavalry detachments made contact with the cavalry on Wellington's left flank. But the main body of the corps was experiencing enormous difficulty. The crossing of the Dyle, the narrow lanes in Wavre and the fire that broke out on the Place Du Sablon (today the Place Bosch) meant a lot of wasted time. The rearguard reached Chapelle-Saint-Lambert towards three in the afternoon.

Progress was extremely difficult along the two possible routes. The first two of Bülow's brigades went into action with his cavalry near Plancenoit at about 4 pm, and the other two followed suit at six. A brigade of Zieten's joined Wellington's left flank at half past seven, and Pirch was able to provide a brigade to support Bülow with effect from eight. Most of the cavalry was engaged in the pursuit. All in all, only 47,000 Prussians took part in the Battle of Waterloo, 19,000 of whom hardly saw action. But this was enough to tip the scales in Wellington's favour.

Grouchy arrived before Wavre towards half past three that afternoon and received the letter that Soult had written at ten. The chief of staff informed him that Wavre was the objective for his right wing and that he had to ensure that he maintained contact with Napoleon. The marshal was delighted that he had not followed Gérard's advice. He entrusted the former task to the 3$^{rd}$ and 4$^{th}$ corps, and gave Pajol and Teste the job of maintaining the link to Napoleon once they were across the Dyle at Limal.

Thielmann made judicious use of the terrain in positioning his troops. The Dyle is a small river that runs through a comparatively wide valley sixty metres below a plateau with fairly steep sides. Ditches and rows of trees bordered the fields. After the heavy rain the river was in flood. The little town of Wavre, which had about 4,000 inhabitants at the time, was situated mainly on the left bank. Two stone bridges connected the town with the district on the other bank. To the north there was the relatively wide Pont du Christ bridge and to the south, the smaller Pont du Moulin. Colonel von Zeppelin had fortified the town and Luck's brigade controlled the Brussels road. The Prussians had destroyed the wooden bridge downstream at Basse-Wavre and were holding the other wooden bridges upstream — Wolf von Stülpnagel's brigade at Bierges and Stengel's 1,200 men at Limal and Limelette. Kemphen's brigade had taken up position to the north-west of Wavre and Hohe's cavalry was posted near the Château de la Bawette, where Thielmann had established himself. With some 18,000 men and 34 guns the Prussian general was preparing to receive the onslaught of an enemy twice as strong.

At 4 o'clock Vandamme brought Habert's division forward for a frontal assault on the town. The eastern part fell without too much difficulty and the French even succeeded in taking the Pont du Christ, but they soon had to take cover from the heavy Prussian fire. But since the attack by the 3rd corps did not produce the hoped-for success, Grouchy gave the order to take the town via Bierges and Basse-Wavre.

Towards five o'clock that afternoon — or was it seven, nobody really knows — Grouchy received a new order from Soult telling him to move in towards the Emperor to crush Bülow's corps. The marshal immediately despatched Pujol's and de Maurin's cavalry and Teste's, Pêcheux's and Vichery's divisions to the Limal bridge. During the attack on the Bierges bridge Gérard was hit in the chest. Grouchy offered the command of the 4th corps to General Baltus, who refused to accept it. So Grouchy led the attack himself, but it also failed.

Towards seven o'clock in the evening the French succeeded in seizing the Limal bridge, and the bridge at Limelette fell shortly afterwards. Two hours later they reached the plateau on the left bank. Further away to the west the gunfire had ceased. The French were optimistic; they thought that the Emperor had beaten the British and that he would make a triumphant entrance into Brussels the following day.

*Following pages :*
*A panoramic view of*
*the Waterloo battlefield.*

Towards eleven o'clock that night Grouchy's men bivouacked hardly 200 metres from the Prussians. They had reached the Rixensart wood and were some 500 metres from Bierges; Vandamme was still stuck in Wavre.

Having learnt of the result of the Battle of Waterloo during the night, Thielmann decided to take the initiative again at dawn.

Grouchy, who was still unaware of the course that events had taken, resolved to outflank Wavre from the west, and so to complete his success as dawn broke. He ordered Vandamme to move towards the left but to keep his campfires burning in order to deceive the enemy into thinking that his troops were still there. Vandamme carried out the order incompletely, moving only two of his four divisions and Exelmans' cavalry. In the morning the Prussians failed in an attempted cavalry attack launched from the Rixensart wood.

Towards half past ten in the morning Grouchy's troops reached the Wavre-Brussels road. La Bawette and the Bois de Rosières wood were in French hands. Thielmann's corps was in full retreat in the direction of Brussels. It was at this point, however, that Grouchy learnt of the result of the Battle of Waterloo. The news was brought by Soult's ADC, but the fact that he had no written orders led to some initial doubt. However they rapidly found themselves having to face facts and decide what to do next. Vandamme suggested pushing on towards Brussels to rescue the prisoners and disrupt the British line of communication, and then to return to France via Enghien, Ath, Valenciennes and Lille. Soult's ADC had added that Grouchy was to withdraw in the direction of the Sambre, and this appeared to be both the logical and the sensible thing to do. The Namur bridges — 40 kms away — had therefore to be seized as soon as possible. Grouchy decided to retreat via Namur, Dinant and Givet.

At half past eleven Exelmans' cavalry received the order to make for Namur as quickly as possible. The dragoons were to seize the bridges over the Meuse and the Sambre. The main body of troops was to retreat in two columns: on the left, the 3$^{rd}$ corps and the 20$^{th}$ Dragoons would proceed via Dion-le-Mont, Tourinnes and Grand-Leez; on the right, the 4$^{th}$ corps under Vichery would take care of the wounded and march via Corbais, Walhain, Gembloux and Temploux. The eastern flank would be covered by Vallin's cavalry. As for Pajol's cavalry, it would form the rearguard with Teste's division and maintain contact with the Prussians.

The retreat took place without provoking any reaction from Thielmann. Karl von Clausewitz, his chief of staff, had stood the troops down until 5 am on the 20$^{th}$! But Pirch left Plancenoit with most of his 2$^{nd}$ corps to cut off Grouchy's retreat. Towards eleven in the evening of the 18$^{th}$ he set off for Bousval and at eleven the following morning he reached Mellery, where his exhausted troops spent the rest of the day and the following night.

At four in the afternoon of the 19$^{th}$ two regiments of French dragoons arrived in Namur. They immediately seized the bridges and the town gates. Three hours later the rest of Exelman's cavalry rode through. At about the same time Grouchy and the 4$^{th}$ corps arrived in Temploux, barely ten kilometres away. On the 20$^{th}$ the first French troops left Namur at six in the morning.

Despite orders the advance guard of the 3$^{rd}$ corps had marched towards Gembloux, where it arrived at about nine in the evening. The rearguard of the corps left the town at 5 am on the 20$^{th}$.

Prussian cavalry regiments were soon being reported everywhere — at Mazy, at Rhisnes, and so on. Were the French encircled? Fighting broke out along the Namur-Nivelles road. Skirmishes reopened the road to Falise. The Prussians' progress was fortunately slowed down by their looting.

A certain Bismarck — a member of the future Chancellor's family — was killed during a clash in Namur. Towards eight o'clock in the evening the last French left the town under the command of the Belgian lieutenant Borremans of the 75$^{th}$ Infantry, a regiment of Teste's division.

On 21$^{st}$ Grouchy's troops crossed the frontier and arrived at Charlemont and Givet, with its fortress on the Mont d'Or. The marshal had succeeded in escaping destruction together with some 28,000 men, all his artillery, his standards, his equipment and numerous wounded,

# CHAPTER X

# Napoleon abdicates

Napoleon arrived in Philippeville at 9 am on June 19th. Having quartered himself in an inn called the *Auberge d'Or* he ordered the troops to assemble at Laon. In the meanwhile he learnt that Ney had left for Paris. Did the Emperor fear a repetition of 1814?

Napoleon left Philippeville in Soult's carriage at about one in the afternoon. After a brief halt in Laon he reached the Elysée on the 21st June at six in the morning. Parliament immediately adopted an attitude of hostility towards him. Davout, Carnot and Lucien Bonaparte advised him to dissolve parliament and to seize power, but he hesitated. The following day he was forced to abdicate in favour of his son, the King of Rome. A provisional government under Joseph Fouché took over the management of current affairs, with Davout once again as Minister of War. Napoleon retired to Malmaison.

On the 24th June 27,000 men had already regrouped in Laon. But defeat, and particularly Napoleon's abdication, had undermined their morale. The previous day Grouchy had been appointed commander in chief of the Northern Army, whose numbers would soon rise to 55,000 men. With this army the

*On the deck of the*
**Northumberland** *en route for St. Helena (MRA collection).*

marshal was able to slow down the Prussian advance. He fought some minor actions at Compiègne, Senlis and Villers-Cotterêts. The British advanced slowly via Péronne and Montdidier. On 29th the Northern Army was in Paris. Blücher succeeded in crossing the Seine near Saint Germain. On 1st July Exelmans defeated the Prussian advance guard at Vélizy.

On 3rd July Davout signed the Convention of Saint Cloud and promised the allies to withdraw the French armies beyond the Loire. Fouché's government recognised Louis XVIII and, on the 7th July, the Prussians marched into Paris. The following day Louis XVIII entered his capital again.

# CHAPTER XI

# By way of a conclusion

## The causes of Napoleon's defeat

**T**he result of the conflict was foreseeable. Even if Napoleon had won the battle of Waterloo it is highly unlikely that his enemies would have granted him any respite. In the long run, Napoleon did not stand the slightest chance in the face of his numerous and resolute enemies, who would stop at nothing to get rid of him. After all, didn't he propagate the utterly detestable ideas of the French revolution and their associated French imperialism ? Napoleon offended against the principle of the relation that the means must bear to the aim.

In 1815 Napoleon no longer had the freedom of action that he had had in the past. A victory was vital if he was to win over the people and, principally, a recalcitrant parliament. Also, he was obliged to appoint certain generals to obtain the allegiance of the traditional aristocracy and the renegades of 1814.

The best results were not always obtained because of the failings of the cavalry, which was incapable of gathering the intelligence that was required. On several occasions Napoleon

*Major Heylant's cenotaph, now in the garden of the Wellington Museum in Waterloo. (Lithograph by Adam, after Pingret, MRA collection).*

wasted time because of the inefficiency of the commissariat and the inadequacy of his staff. Cooperation between the different arms — artillery, infantry and cavalry — was far from perfect and communications non-existent. And lastly Waterloo, the site of the main battle, was imposed by Wellington. The battle heralded a period of 125 years during which tactics would be dominated by defence.

## Wellington overwhelmed with honours — and Property

In 1814 France had had to relinquish the territorial gains that she had made after 1792. The Second Treaty of Paris of 20th November 1815 imposed an indemnity of 700 million francs to be paid to the allies. Seven northern *départements* were occupied by the allies at French expense. The country lost 525,000 inhabitants. The region including Solre-sur-Sambre, Beaumont, Walcourt, Florennes, Philippeville, Mariembourg, Chimay, Couvin and Bouillon was allocated to the Kingdom of the Netherlands. Prussia received Saarbrücken and Saarlouis, Ney's home town. The town of Landau went to Bavaria, and Savoy to the King of Sardinia. Only Savoy would return to France, in 1860. Even after 1918 and 1945 the Saar and Landau would not become French again.

Britain's prosperity increased after 1811 due to the failure of the Continental System. And the economic boom after 1815 increased it even more. But the situation changed in 1819, and particularly since there were 200,000 or so soldiers and sailors who were now unemployed.

The banker Nathan Rothschild was most certainly the person who profited most from Waterloo. The official news of the victory reached London on 21$^{st}$ June. It is probable that Nathan had received the news (by carrier pigeon?) as early as the 19$^{th}$, when London was still alarmed at the result of the battles of Quatre-Bras and Ligny. When Nathan Rothschild sold a block of shares, a large number of other investors followed suit. Some hours before the news of the victory became known Nathan bought up a large amount of stock at very favourable rates. And made a profit of a million pounds in the process.

Wellington was overwhelmed with honours — and property. In 1817 the British Parliament presented him with the Stratfield Saye estate. Not content with granting him the title of Prince of Waterloo, the Kingdom of the Netherlands allocated him an annual pension of 21,000 florins, the proceeds from an endowment of 1,083 hectares of woodland. Under the *ancien régime* most of this land — lying in the districts of Nivelles,

*Major Heylant's grave today.*

Thines, Obaix, Frasnes, Baisy and Genappe — had belonged to the Chapter of Sainte Gertrude in Nivelles, the Abbey of Affligem and the Knights of Malta. As no purchasers had been found after its nationalisation in 1795, the government could dispose of it as it saw fit. After obtaining the authorisation of the Kingdom of the Netherlands Wellington had the trees felled in 1817. Invested in shares, the interest in 1872 was 80,106 francs and, adjusted to take account of the effects of inflation, this sum still comes out of the Belgian government's annual budget today. However, the real profit comes from the several millions of francs paid to the Duke's descendants by the farmers working this land. Since the property cannot be sold as long as there are direct male descendants of the Duke, the farmers will continue to enjoy a high degree of stability. The Belgian government will assume ownership should the male line die out.

Wellington was appointed field marshal in the Prussian, Russian, Austrian, Spanish and Portuguese armies and drew the corresponding emoluments. Wellington's *cursus honorum* did not stop in 1815. From 1828 to 1830 he even headed a Tory government. He was vigorously opposed to the Reform Bill and had iron shutters installed after the windows of Aspley House, his private residence, had been stoned — hence his nickname "The Iron Duke". In 1846 he retired from politics and died on 14th February 1852 in his 83rd year. He rests in St. Paul's Cathedral in London. Blücher, who was also overwhelmed with honours, died in 1819 aged 77.

France had to pay fifty million francs war reparations to be shared out equally between the British and the Prussians. Wellington had the British share distributed among the soldiers of his army. Those from the Kingdom of the Netherlands, Hanover, Brunswick and Nassau also received their share. Where death had intervened, the money went to the heirs. Generals received 30,589 francs, senior officers 10,394, captains 2,168, lieutenants 833, sergeants 461 and the rank and file 61. This was known as the Waterloo gratuity.

In a Royal Decree of the 9<sup>th</sup> November 1815 William I made provision for pensions to be paid to invalids, widows and orphans. This piece of social legislation was financed from a special fund set up for the purpose. The money came from donations, a government contribution, and what remained from the Waterloo gratuities, i.e. the sums not claimed by soldiers of the Kingdom of the Netherlands or their heirs. The most urgent cases requiring action as the result of hostilites benefited from a gift of 50,000 francs donated by William I. The sovereign also had food taken out of military stores. A commisson set up by the Royal Decree of 15<sup>th</sup> July 1815 examined complaints and distributed subsidies and gifts to help those most in need.

On the 26<sup>th</sup> March 1914 Georges Helleputte, the Catholic Minister of Agriculture and Public Works, undertook to classify the battlefield following Hector Fleischmann's initiative. Quick action took the liberals in the Chamber by surprise, but in the Senate they appealed to the sacrosanct right to property. The overwhelming Catholic majority imposed its will, however. The site — which cannot be modified in any way — extends over some 500 hectares from the Mont Saint Jean farm in the north to the Aigle Blessé in the south. In the east, the boundary

*The monuments to Colonel Gordon and the Hanoverians. (Lithograph by Willaume, MRA collection).*

155

passes through Fichtermont and in the west, along the Nivelles road.

The idea of classifying the battlefield developed in anticipation of the hundredth anniversary of the battle in 1915. But the planned festivities were swept away by another war ! However, the name of Waterloo has lost nothing of its allure. More than 130 towns, villages and other places now bear this name in Britain and her erstwhile colonies, particularly Canada. The name also occurs in the United States and Germany. Some villages in Germany are called *La Belle Alliance*. However, since the end of the Second World War the Germans have also been won over to the name of Waterloo.

# Bibliography

We do not see much point in listing all the books, articles and archives, etc. that we consulted in producing this book.

Concerning the troops of the Kingdom of the Netherlands, the best work to date remains F. DE BAS & J. DE T'SERCLAES' *La campagne de 1815 aux Pays-Bas* in three volumes with maps, Albert Dewit, Brussels 1909. BIKAR, ANDRÉ *Les Belges à Waterloo* in the Revue Internationale d'Histoire Militaire No. 24, 1965, pps. 365-392. A recent publication in English from my Sandhurst colleague D. CHANDLER is *Waterloo, The Hundred Days*, Osprey, London, 1980, 224 pp. The most complete work in French is that of J. THIRY *La chute de Napoléon I. La première abdication. Le vol de l'Aigle. Les cent jours. Waterloo. La Seconde abdication.* 7 volumes, Paris, 1938-1945.

# Contents